MISTAKES TO RUN WITH

Yasuko Thanh

MISTAKES TO
RUN WITH

HAMISH HAMILTON

an imprint of Penguin Canada, a division of Penguin Random House Canada Limited

Canada • USA • UK • Ireland • Australia • New Zealand • India • South Africa • China

First published 2019

www.penguinrandomhouse.ca

LIBRARY AND ARCHIVES CANADA CATALOGUING IN PUBLICATION

Thanh, Yasuko, author
Mistakes to run with : a memoir / Yasuko Thanh.

Issued in print and electronic formats.
ISBN 978-0-7352-3441-3 (softcover).—ISBN 978-0-7352-3442-0 (electronic)

1. Thanh, Yasuko. 2. Thanh, Yasuko—Childhood and youth.
3. Authors, Canadian (English)—British Columbia—Biography. I. Title.

PS8639.H375Z466 2019   C813'.6   C2018-902404-6
                                               C2018-902405-4

Cover design: Terri Nimmo
Cover images: (front) Alex Waber (back) Picsfive / Shutterstock.com

Printed and bound in Canada

10 9 8 7 6 5 4 3 2 1

Penguin
Random House
HAMISH HAMILTON CANADA

For my children

All memory . . . is memory for something.
PATRICK GEARY

PART I

WHEEL OF REBIRTH

VANCOUVER, 1988. I'm seventeen, sitting on an overturned milk crate in the July heat.

My best friend Frances rubbed her toes through the leather of her stilettos. She was black, half Native, and didn't know her real father. People said his name was Fergie and that he was from Barbados. This is all anyone knew.

Although Frances was prettier than the other girls on the track, Japanese dates rarely took her out. No matter that she spoke a little of their language, learned while working at Bradley's nightclub, which catered to Asian businessmen with thick wallets. If she and I were out on the corner together, chances were I'd catch a date first.

My hot-pink tube top shimmered in the sun. I sucked a frozen strawberry juice bar, monitoring my tan through my sunglasses. I'd flung my six-inch heels aside; they lay in the shadow of the Korner

Kitchen coffee shop. I slathered my legs with baby oil, careful not to spill any on my miniskirt.

Five years before, the local newspaper in Victoria, British Columbia, where I grew up, had published an article about my academic, athletic, and civic achievements. My place on the school math team had earned us a spot in the Gauss Contest. I'd won a French public-speaking competition that sent provincial finalists to Ottawa to meet the Governor General, Jeanne Sauvé. The article featured a grainy picture I hated: skinny face, acne, poodle perm. My parents had saved the clipping and, before gluing it into the pages of a family scrapbook, had sent photocopies to aunts and uncles in Europe.

"I need at least four today," Frances said. Her pimp wasn't known for setting quotas. I figured she had rent to pay.

I'd already made three hundred dollars that morning and stashed the money in my bra, where the folded bills scratched against my breasts.

Frances often worked double shifts to earn what I did in three hours. At the age of seventeen I was convinced of the righteousness of my behaviour, which showed what a person could do when not intimidated. I ate lobster, drove a Camaro. I wasn't a victim. We smiled from the curb at the men who drove around the block, waved, beckoned with our index fingers, manufacturing a sweetness for even the circle jerks who ogled our flesh through their car windows but never stopped to take us out. This was part of the job, smiling while covering up our fear.

At the age of fifteen, within the space of two months, I'd gone from losing my virginity to performing half-and-halfs on the street that cost two hundred bucks, half blow job, half lay. Another year of work had brought me to Vancouver, to this point now, deep in the summer of 1988.

I'd never had a violent date like Frances who'd been kidnapped, bound with rope, held captive in a garage, and forced to eat dog food before being set free two days later. Another friend had been attacked, her head split open, by a guy driving a station wagon with a child's car seat in the back. She'd tried to block the blows while yelling she was pregnant but he beat her unconscious with his crowbar anyway. I saw her in the Korner Kitchen two weeks later: she'd returned to work with her arm in a cast and seventy-two stitches in her head.

I remember thinking I was lucky. I remember thinking I was careful. Such things could never happen to me.

Fortunes of All Humans

The previous year, in September 1987 when I was sixteen, a
psychologist wrote to my probation officer in my case file:
"Her responses on the Rorschach are the type of responses that
might be expected from a neglected and deprived child and leave
me wondering about the adequacy of care that has been provided
by her parents, even in the most basic physical areas."

In a city known for its trees, I grew up on a street with none.
Victoria, 1974. My father, a Vietnamese national who spoke four
languages and had a degree from a Parisian university, found work
in a shoe store, a far cry from the financial industry and the bank
he'd thought would employ him. Before immigrating to British
Columbia and settling on the west coast he'd studied business
management. He'd met my mother in Europe when he was twenty-
seven and she was sixteen. Handsome as Bruce Lee, he promised a
ticket away from her home in dour grey postwar Germany. They

6

came to Canada in 1970, a year before I was born. My mother had fantasized about riding escalators in glamorous North American shopping malls, but what greeted her in Victoria during those heady days of Trudeaumania was more grey. Rain. A rooming house. More rain. My father found himself walking to the shoe store next to a bowling alley to sell pumps to women who couldn't understand his thick accent and asked him to repeat "What size do you take?" My mother still spoke to me in German at home. During the afternoons, when the sun shone on our balcony, we played school. She practised the English phrases she'd heard on TV while I sat cross-legged next to her, writing "Mama, do you love me?" in an orange exercise book.

When my brother was born, in the winter of 1976, my parents gave him my room. I was relegated to a flip chair—*Her responses leave me wondering about the adequacy of care*—that unfolded into a kid's bed a few feet from the front door. I didn't understand why I had to give him anything, to share anything. Why didn't they put *him* in the living room? Or in the kitchen? Better yet, why couldn't they take him back to wherever he'd come from? I'd trade him in for a Barbie doll.

When my parents needed the living room to watch a movie or the news, they put me to sleep in their bed. I once squirted my mother's nose drops onto her pillow to wet it the way tears would so she'd know I was sad. My mother didn't notice the wetness; or, if she did, she said nothing about it the next day.

It shouldn't have surprised me. Comfort was a foreign currency in my family. If I was upset, my father would splash my face with water cold enough to take my breath away. This much I knew: voicing unpleasant emotions made you unlovable. My craving for acceptance and my inability to express my need made me misbehave; my father would spank me with a thick wooden ruler. My mother's slaps, they at least touched me. I must be a bad girl, I thought, yet I didn't understand why. My parents' expectations of me were as baffling as they were mutable. All day I would follow the rules to have my mother confront me at bedtime with a list of sins I'd committed without knowing it.

In the years to come I would give them perfect report cards, ribbons won at track, certificates of academic achievement. I went to church and volunteered, spoon-fed boys and girls crippled with cerebral palsy at the Queen Alexandra hospital. I'd bring home these offerings yet saw no reason to be proud of my achievements. Perfection was expected. Not praised.

For my entire childhood—and still, today, part of me waits— I'd needed to hear three simple words from my parents: You Are Good. Good. Worthy. Valuable. You are valuable to me. You are valuable to the rest of the world. Not because of what you do but because you are you, inherently important to us. You are not a bad girl. You are *good*.

I plotted revenge against my brother, and would pinch him to make him cry. But there was something else. I pinched him not to hurt but to comfort him, so that I'd have a reason to pick him up, dry his tears. Whisper, "Hush, hush, hush."

To escape my confusion I'd often play outside our apartment building near where the grass ended and the road into our housing project began. There the grass grew tallest and the St. John's wort was bushy enough to act as a forest.

I had one doll—my father had inexplicably thrown away all my toys when the rest of us weren't home—and my favourite game was doctor. I inflicted Barbie with injuries, scrawled blood drops with red ballpoint. One day, when I was five or six, I decided to run away. Woolco would be a good, safe place to go, lots of toys, bright lights, a Popsicle machine. I knew the way down the road that circled our building toward a busy six-lane street. A friend's mother saw me on the road, fiddling with my doll, and invited me to their apartment for a cup of tea. She felt sorry for me. I drank the tea instead of running away, enjoying how much sugar I could use, when helping myself, to sweeten my cup.

I finished the tea and went back outside. I found an abandoned construction site. Standing atop a pile of wood I became Queen of the Two-by-Four, Queen of Nails, Queen of Drywall. I picked out my bedroom and showed my doll hers. It was all there in plywood and rebar—the framework to a happy life.

Years passed. My parents' tenacity and dreams gave way to disappointment—misfortune has a way of misering its victims. My mother did not get her promised yearly trip home to visit her six brothers and sisters; it was out of the question. Winter rains ushered in mud puddles and a road wet with oil slicks. My mother told me later that in those years she dreamed of running away across the rooftops of our neighbourhood, clutching a suitcase in one hand and my hand in the other, my brother on her hip as we escaped. It haunted her.

The nights my father worked late, my mother, brother, and I occupied the chesterfield, bolstered by pillows my mother had made herself. The awkwardness that blossomed between us as I grew dissolved when we watched TV. Sometimes I even pretended to fall asleep because when I did my mother would smooth back my hair and kiss me.

We didn't live in absolute poverty, only the relative sort. My classmates had money for nail polish and velour sweaters from Woodward's; they went to movies, slept in a bed, rode a bike. I did these things too, but much later than everyone else.

At eight years old I'd take the bus to the Y downtown. Every Saturday I saw other parents dropping off their children, but I never expected a ride. I'd sit in the seat to the right of the bus driver reserved for people with mobility issues. I'd look forward to chatting with him. He asked lots of questions.

Forty years have gone by since the two photographs were taken that I withdraw from a shoebox and place before me, their corners yellowed. It's difficult to reconcile the images I see of myself in old photographs with how I felt at the time.

A crack runs through one of them: I'm nine or ten, turning a cartwheel on matted grass. I have on the red vest with pink crosses that my mother had knitted me. I remember disliking the vest but wearing it anyway, guilty about not loving it more. In the photograph my mother hunkers ten feet back, watching me from the front steps in sunglasses, a shiny blouse. She cups her chin—no, *mashes* it—against her cheek. It is the face of a general, grimacing, frowning.

My mother loved the idea of hope, feeding it with more dreams than it could swallow. By now she'd taken up with an evangelical God, telling the Christian stories of resilience—mouth painters who'd become quadriplegic in horrible accidents, Holocaust survivors—that filled my childhood. She inducted me into the Pentecostal army of God with a vengeance, and I complied enthusiastically.

My mother was like someone behind glass that divided her from me, froze her gaze. Yet I fantasized that beneath her cold blue eyes she had a fire, an inner Mrs. Brady, because I'd once turned my head to see her turn her own cartwheel. In that moment of laughter I saw her spirit. Somewhere in there another woman, the happy version of my mother, was trapped and trying to get out.

We moved from the apartment to a townhouse down the street. I was entering grade three, eight years old. I don't remember packing. I don't remember moving trucks. What I remember is walking through the empty new house followed by the echo of my footsteps. What legroom and breathing space smelled like. The dresser left behind in one of the rooms was antique—I took the drawers out, examining their workmanship. Why? Because that piece of furniture would reveal something about the earlier occupants. I found a handwritten receipt with a 1940s date on it.

The townhouse had three bedrooms, a tiny yard; it faced a playground with a concrete elephant covered in graffiti, a swing set on which older kids would sit after I'd gone to bed. I could hear their hoots and hollers through my window, their robust party yells. The sound of breaking glass after they'd lobbed an empty bottle—I imagined the high arc of some smooth, clear, exotic bird following its own trajectory through the night to inevitably, thrillingly, crash down to earth, strike the asphalt, and explode in a rainbow prism of glass that I'd sidestep the following day as I played. All I had to do was show my face in this community space separated from the adult world by an invisible force field, sacred ground preordained for small feet alone, and approach a kid. "Wanna play?"

For the next hour we'd pretend that only these swings, this gnarly apple tree, this concrete elephant existed. This tree is a fort. The ground is covered in snakes. You can't go down or you'll be eaten. These apples are grenades. Launch them at the boys.

These days, having my own room means survival in a world that presses in. My own room is the bubble that surrounds me; I retreat there when the pressures of the world get to be too much as if into a diving bell under a hundred feet of ocean. If I sense a crack, I seal it up by halting communication with the outside.

Sometimes the space contracts around me, mordant, until the sound of my own breathing swallows me. The awareness that what protects me sanctions my survival doesn't stave off the ensuing claustrophobia. The patient in an oxygen tent still hates her immobility. Her weakness. The sickness that put her there in the first place. She wishes she could get up and walk through the transparent walls—beyond them she can see others living their lives—yet what she's suffered makes this impossible. Any outside contact carries the potential of a fatal infection. So the patient learns to live with her lot. Learns to appreciate her separateness.

Back then, before having my own room, my own setting to house the items symbolically meaningful to me, I'd choose a section of hallway in the apartment, between the living room and the bathroom, and lay out the books I'd withdrawn from the library earlier that day in a row. My own room meant I could do the same thing but in private, with more than books. I took meticulous care in arranging every object I owned. Tiny plastic animals the dentist gave away after an appointment, ceramic figurines from tea boxes, my stuffed animals, my dolls—each had a location, a private corner they didn't have to share with anyone.

I also had my own closet, which, small as it was, stood for another world, separated from my room with its own door. Though not large enough for me to play in, I'd shrink myself to fit the space, contort enough to allow the door to at least shut behind me. In that sanctuary I'd fend off attacks from my little brother, who would often invade my room with the force of an advancing army. This was the universe's way of preparing me for that haven's forfeiture, not to my brother but to my grandparents, who will be sponsored by my father in a few years' time. They will take my room. I'll move in with my brother. Then, after another few years, they'll move to France where my aunt and uncle live, where they will stay until they die.

A few weeks or months after moving in I got my first real bed, with captain's drawers that slid out from under the mattress, all my clothes folded and placed inside. Like an interior designer I'd sit back and look at the tableau of my neatly made bed, my fluffed pillows. Ponder. Absorb. Rearrange. Able to stop only when it felt "right."

It never did.

Even then the clash between the blue-painted wall and the olive carpet, between my mismatched bedding and the wall papered burgundy, disrupted the peace I was trying to cultivate.

Kitchen Gods and Flying Ghosts

My parents had no friends to stay for coffee and accept biscuits, litter the table with crumbs, leave dishes in the sink. More than anything I wanted to fit in, but I could count on my fingers the number of times I'd stayed for dinner at a friend's house or asked a playmate over after school. While my friends spent weekends in each other's rec rooms, living out of their sleeping bags, eating popcorn, watching movies, I sat alone in my room and made up stories. In those stories I talked with ease about Luke Skywalker, or the best games to play at Chuck E. Cheese's, or how it felt to have your ears pierced.

In the other photograph, I am five. I point to my own grin, delighted by my birthday cake. Strawberries, five candles. My mother's hands rest on the shoulders of my sundress, and she manages to smile to hide her sadness just now when my father snaps the photo.

Although I appear bold and fearless in these photos, at that time I still wet my bed or awoke crying for no reason. Photos of family camping trips and Christmas trees, Santa's lap, and bicycle outings don't show my misery. When worried or afraid I'd scratch my arms raw, looking for answers beneath the first layer of skin. But in snapshots of me roller-skating down the street, or surrounded by fall leaves, or sitting in snow at my mother's side, all you can see is my smile. How do I reconcile the ribbons my parents saved with their absence from those races won or lost? How to reconcile my smile in those pictures with the sorrow I know I felt?

Sadness coexisted with happiness like rats in the walls of a house—trapped but staying hidden, and in that darkness continuing to breed. I knew a secret loneliness, triggered at the age of five or six by a realization that hit me with the power of a tsunami. I'd been sitting in the kitchen, looking at one parent, then the other. I was separate, alone in the universe. I was coming to understand that you had a whole long life to live but you'd never be able to see the world through anyone else's eyes. No matter how badly I wanted it, I could never know what other people were thinking. Indescribable sadness came with registering the vast distances between each of us, a sadness that has stayed with me in variations to this day.

The summer I was six I filled a fifty-page notebook with my first novel. Loneliness spurred the writing, but the release it bestowed kept me at it. In writing, I didn't have to be lonely. I could be whoever I wanted, see the world through anyone's eyes. Writing emulated the interpersonal; I could write friends into the plot— go to as many sleepovers as I chose. I wrote about a parade, a dress-up contest, a girl who raises money for the March of Dimes. Though writing was different from love, when I inhabited my characters on the page connection occurred, acting as the balm I needed.

Fall, 1978. I am seven years old. I watch my neighbour's dirty fingers, rounded at the tips, sorting through the candy in the salad bowl. He and I huddle together on the steps of the apartment building. Shawn is eight and his hair is defiant and unruly, not like mine, bone straight and serious. His older brother Sully sits with his arms loose around his knees.

I write as though I'm writing about someone else. "I" is an invention to prove we exist. "I" is the line drawn through the fabric of time. "I" imposes meaning on random events. "I" implies significance.

I jam three Allsorts and two wine gums into my pocket.

Unlike me, both brothers stuff their candy into their mouths. Sometimes we make candy salads out of what we've begged going door to door. Shawn twists his face to the sun. He and his brother astonish me with their beauty. Some kids call Sully with his pigeon toes a cripple and they think Shawn's eyes are oddly wide-set, but I disagree.

"When I grow up," I say, "I'm gonna give candy to anyone who asks."

"That's just stupid," Shawn says.

My stomach tingles when Shawn speaks. But now I snatch the bowl.

"*You're* stupid." With a focused urgency, knowing they're watching me, I run away from them. Life gains on me but I won't stop to look back.

———

The next day I look for Shawn and find him puttering by the swing set. When he sees me I offer him my most winning smile and twirl on one foot, my hands folded behind my back. Shawn can switch from fun to mean in a second. I've seen it. He has something inside him, wild as a feral cat, familiar yet frightening, that I want to harness.

I wrap my fist around yesterday's candies still in my pocket. Rub them, then reluctantly release them. "You want to learn how to fly?" I ask.

I lead him to the staircase next to our suite, climb up and balance on the inside of the railing, fifteen feet above the grass. I sweep my leg out over it. He watches me and waits.

When I leap out, away from the staircase, I imagine his gaping mouth, his awe and shock, heavy as a star launched out of the heavens, but when I hear him race down the stairs toward me I want to hide.

I've landed bent double and can only wipe the hair from my eyes, spit it out of my mouth.

The moment he touches my shoulder I force myself to stand. I slap my palms together to brush off the grass.

"Are you okay?" he asks.

I will not let him see me cry. "Loser," I say, limping toward the stairs to catch my breath. I wish I'd flown. As I laugh through my tears, I wish I'd made Shawn wish he'd flown as well.

"I'm bored," Shawn says. "*Aren't you?*" He challenges, admonishes me the way a parent would.

First I think we're going to go begging candy door to door again, but we end up at the corner store down the street. If I stick with Shawn things will happen to me.

In the cool darkness of the shop Shawn fingers rubber balls, candy cigarettes, jawbreakers. I slip a grape Lik-a-Stix into my pocket. We walk out of the store, expecting to run away whooping, the owner trying to grab us, but nothing happens.

We find a spot up the block where I smear my lips with the stolen purple powder. I pass it to Shawn and watch the powder dissolve to a plum-coloured stain. I think of clowns and laugh.

Shawn leads me to the playground at the bottom of the ravine. The swings and the slide are tangled in morning glory vines that snake up over the teeter-totter. I pull at the collar of my T-shirt. Summer gets in anyway, hot and sticky as molasses. Shawn swats at mosquitoes.

He marks the air with his pee in a yellow arc the shape of a rainbow. Some lands on leaves and ants scurry. I wonder if they think it's raining.

After he stops he tells me to pee, too, and when I'm done he pushes me down and climbs on top of me. Dead leaves and moss on the flat rock chill my bare bum. He rubs his body against mine. The rock chills my back, dampens it. He closes his eyes as he bucks. I'm not sure whether I like this game or not.

I look over by the bushes where the creek bed rises and meanders into sloping yards. Today a man is sitting on a plastic lawn chair. I want to say "I think we should get out of here," but Shawn traps my hips beneath the vise of his legs, which are unbelievably strong, and his face stretches into a smirk.

I stay home for seven days. On the eighth day I hang around the staircase, the landing from where I flew, hoping to bump into Shawn.

I wind down the path to the ravine playground. When at last I'm sure I'll never see him again, he appears by the monkey bars.

The night before, I dreamed of him. I dreamed of his hand in mine, then I dreamed of flying off the staircase and away, my wings as strong as a hawk's.

His brother Sully joins us and before they can leave me, before they can walk away, I tempt them by asking, "How strong do you think I am?"

Shawn shrugs. I'm just a girl acting stupid.

But Sully regards me with curiosity and sits down. Painted stones perch side by side and the three of us sit like crows on a wire.

"Stronger than you."

Sully's eyes twinkle yet he turns away, whistles through his teeth. "Strong?" he says. "Right."

Shawn jumps me unexpectedly. We wrestle on the warm grass, which makes my stomach tingle in the same way as when I listen to him speak or watch him eat stolen candy. But he can't win. Not like this.

I push him off. "Bet I can break your *finger*," I say.

They laugh.

"Yeah, right," Shawn says. "Try it."

He extends his hand and I grab the middle finger with all the strength I have.

He snatches his hand out of my grasp. "Ha!"

Sully can't stop giggling.

Shawn smiles, self-satisfied. "Betcha I can break yours," he says.

Am I pouting? Teasing? Part of me wishes I could draw my knees to my chest, say "I don't want to." The other part needs his touch.

"Or maybe you think I'm not *strong* enough?"

I stretch open my hand but it's Sully who takes it. Someday, looking at it from the outside, I'll postulate how our experiences became the net that surrounded us, separated us from others. What was about to happen, my hand moving toward Sully's, his first grasp tinged with gentleness and friendship, this belonging, was why I'd come. Although in my dream it hadn't happened this way. Sully grabs hold and yanks my middle finger back. Do I hear it snap? Or think I do?

Either way, I now understand that the universe listens. It tries to give us what we wish for—but in a way we don't always expect. Now I know that Sully doesn't love me, and that Shawn never did.

City of Innocent Deaths

Eight years old, sitting in a vinyl chair decorated with flowers, I wrote on a blue typewriter. A suitcase typewriter, hard shelled, white handled, *Smith-Corona* stamped across the front. *Clack-clack-clack*. The satisfying ring at the end of the line, like the bell in the boxing matches my father watched. *Back to your corner*.

If you didn't aim properly your finger would sail past the plastic letter into the machine's metal innards. Accuracy. Speed. A little strength. This is what counted.

I armed myself with discount bottles of Wite-Out. Three mistakes per page—I'd read the rules—or start over. I wrote "How the Leopard Got Its Spots." "Why the Turtle Has a Shell." "The Elephant and Its Trunk."

My grade three teacher sent me to Mrs. Kendrick's grade four class to read, out loud, my story about airplanes, and a war, and a little girl.

I read it to my parents. They asked me if I'd plagiarized it.

When I grew up I could be Harriet the Spy. The recorder, the experience thief. I captured things in a notebook like a spy. I'd pull it out of my back pocket and write down licence plate numbers, describe the clothes people were wearing. Both spies and writers got to be other people, something denied them in real life. Unlike actors, their stakes were higher. More like missionaries who might end up as dinner, dying for their beliefs. Both spying and writing seemed dangerous.

At the library I was always looking over my shoulder—lest an adult should question what someone my age was doing in the windswept women section, the ones who adorned the covers of the Harlequin and Silhouette romance novels I devoured like popcorn. Their plot structure mirrored the affairs themselves: introduction leading to a climax. I learned that if you were beautiful people would trip all over themselves to please you. I could hold my own at street hockey, but being beautiful was a better goal. Why not be worshipped?

I cut images of gymnast Nadia Comăneci from magazines and taped them to the wall. I did handstands on the grass, in my bedroom. I did push-ups and practised the splits. I'd read somewhere that the greatest insult to God was thwarting His dream for you, and I wanted no part of insulting God. God had given me a passion for gymnastics. I was going to honour His gift.

A coach at the Y must have seen me jumping around in the dance room one Saturday and made a few phone calls. Overnight, it looked as if my prayers had been answered. Victoria's best gymnastics program for girls called my parents to say they wanted me to train me—they wanted me!

My parents would have to say yes!

When I heard my father refusing their offer something inside me crumbled like the pages of an old fairy tale when touched, brought into the light. The light shed on my parents revealed their desire to hurt me by taking away my dream. Here, finally, had been proof—that there was someone out there in the world, the gym coach, who *wanted* me. I had no inkling why my parents wanted to sabotage me. A few years later I assumed the lessons had been too expensive. Then, as an adult, I'd learn that my father had been convinced I'd injure myself.

"I wasn't afraid," my mother said, "but he was."

Each time the gym phoned my father turned them down. Not realizing that my life swung in the balance, he ended these intrusions as he'd have hung up on a telemarketer. The calls stopped. Confused, broken-hearted, I took down my pictures of Nadia.

When gymnastics competitions aired on TV I changed the channel.

What could I do?

What *would* I do?

I had to move forward. My conclusion was that the universe wasn't benevolent. Like the rest of nature, it was at best only cruelly indifferent. This forced a couple of truisms to the fore.

One: don't expect anything just for being born.

Two: the best thing you can do is stop asking and start taking. Like a kid in a candy store, this and this and this.

Fill your pockets. Don't look back.

———

Victoria, 1982. I'm eleven years old. I stand in the playground, the centre of a universe swaying with tire swings, the paint flaking from see-saws, green scabs peeling onto the black asphalt, the hum of the thoroughfare beyond the chain-link fence, the blades of grass browning in the sun, the incessant barking of a dog that circles its owner who's muttering in pretend Chinese as he karate-chops the air like Chuck Norris, a June sky and a telephone wire spotted with pigeons, the smell of oil from the white stucco restaurant on the corner as the cook lowers the day's first orders of battered cod into the deep fryer.

In my neighborhood, whether we were playing street hockey, soccer, or conkers, any arena would do when it came to enacting our offensives. Our violence was a form of love, the connection between them woefully clear to me even at eleven. The fighting spirit of my neighbourhood is deeply woven into the fabric of that time, into my understanding of the topology of those dead-end streets.

What will happen to the boy in this story will happen after I've gone to bed and completed all my rituals. I recorded the time for Jesus in my diary. I wrote 9:12 p.m. because it's imperative that I tell the Son of God the precise time. My parents won't love me, even if I hurt myself to make myself more lovable, but God will. When I look at the clock a minute later it's vital to record this too. 9:13 p.m. 9:24 p.m. 9:31 p.m. In between I read passages of my Bible, and then, compelled to touch my curtains a certain number of times, I rock on my bed, repeating "Get thee behind me, Satan"—a line from one of my Christian Crusaders action-duo comics—and look in the mirror to make sure the devil isn't staring back.

In my memory it's the sound that rouses me from sleep. It's so loud the windows rattle, paintings tilt on the wall, a collection of ceramic owls slides off a shelf and shatters. The newspaper accounts will contradict me, saying the explosion (which hasn't yet happened), not the crash, caused the sliding and shattering. The crash was a boy driving into a ditch to go around a roadblock he hadn't expected to be there. But no one's memory is more accurate than your own.

I ran outside and watched with others, watched the boy tumble out of the car with his girlfriend. Years later it's her face I remember, even though this cannot be. The way she cried, mascara running down her cheeks, is a memory I've invented. She wasn't there.

The boy had driven this street so many times he could be forgiven for believing it went straight through. But now in his way stood a barrier of steel and wood, a little gap on one side so that pedestrians could pass. The city had recently erected it, after my father had petitioned for a roadblock, persuaded them to protect us at our games of scrub, soccer, and hockey that spilled onto the street.

The accident still seems like a game to me, with all the excitement of rides on the midway, complete with police lights and the wail of sirens. The boy had a bad reputation; the police would pull him over, subject him to searches, ignore probable cause. He'd been calling the station for days now: he had dynamite in his car, he'd say, and if they didn't stop harassing him he'd blow himself up. Did they see something of themselves in his bravado? Did his youthful defiance provoke their envy? Or did contempt make them dismiss his threats as the cultivated talk of inner-city high school boys? His girlfriend had called the station and so had his father, warning, "Your harassment is pushing him *to the edge*. If you don't stop, something bad's going to happen."

No one listened.

The police drew a tighter circle around him even as he was yelling "If you come any closer, I'll blow myself the fuck up."

I imagine him believing it would never come to this. I imagine him a moment earlier, before the crash, steering a doomed 1966 Plymouth Fury, removing the crucifix from the rear-view mirror and slipping it over his head, driving with his knees, reciting a Hail Mary, streetlights stringing by like rosary beads.

While he waved his dynamite and his girlfriend screamed "*Lethimgobabydon'tdoit*" (in real life she arrived after the explosion, saw his body on the pavement half-blanketed by a tarp), the police lassoed him.

What happened next I wrote in my diary. I kept a diary throughout my childhood, as I kept dead bees in a jar. For their calm, which could be savoured. When the boy exploded, I told my brother how his parts were raining down upon us. Newspaper accounts would make note of the 1966 Plymouth Fury being split in half. The windshield flew the length of an Olympic swimming pool. A skylight was pierced by falling debris a football field away. Seventeen windows were smashed in nearby houses. People felt the blast over a two-kilometre radius.

My brother looked like he was about to cry.

"Right now," I hissed. "Guts like snakes."

If it weren't for this record, there are days when I'd say it never happened. Some of the words in my diary are misspelled.

I ran in my pyjamas through the long grass, looking for body parts. I wanted, needed, to see how the pieces fit.

The boy was like the moth that flies toward the light, and my father was like the light. Someone once said that every action of ours is evil for someone else. What happened to the boy was no one's fault, but that doesn't preclude looking at who made him feel trapped, at how far people will go to recover what's been denied. The palpable innocence connected to the colour of that night, see-saws in the dark, an apple tree against orange flames, the blistering paint, a long-ago June, the summer a lake bed, stretching out—this imagined beauty creates our idiosyncratic illusion of freedom, a concrete means to think about the *sine qua non* of good and evil: that when confronted by a dead end we might be capable of anything.

Chamber of Maggots and
Terrible Bee Torture

Nobody cared enough about me to wonder why I cried myself to sleep at night. Why I tried to make myself sick by ingesting mould I'd cultivated on a three-month-old bread crust. No one asked if I was happy. Or if I was sad. I could do brilliant things or horrible things. No one noticed either way.

I tried to make myself lovable. I picked my mother flowers; she asked whose yard I'd stolen them from.

Overtly, I expressed no hostility toward my father for losing his job, for the way things began to break around the house the year I turned twelve: my father's spirit, his back, and his heart, which he complained about—the weight of shoeboxes he'd lifted and dragged from the stock room to the floor where he arranged them for display.

I was finally old enough for a paper route. After saving enough money I was able, at last, to sign myself up for gymnastics lessons. I couldn't get enough. I trained away the frustration of my father's malingering, his symptoms that changed day to day, trained away the reasons he had to stay in bed. His paranoia. He claimed he could smell from two blocks away the cleanser that a woman, scrubbing her kitchen clean then opening a window to let out the day's burdensome heat, had decided to poison him with, its odour more powerful than a bullet. He said he was dying. He said that even the doctors were trying to kill him.

He thought so, perhaps, because the hospital couldn't find the source of his pain. Still, he'd cough fiercely—stupidly, I thought—at the scent of a carpet, the aroma of roses, new clothing, used clothing. My mother would have to wash an undershirt five times before she could even bring it into the house.

She lost herself in Bible readings, ignoring his deterioration. I watched her pray before meals with her head bent low like a lamb to the slaughter. I had no idea if lambs lowered their heads at slaughter, but it had a nice ring to it. She always ended with "In Jesus's name," the trick for making God aware—the extra stamp on the envelope, the difference between priority post and express.

I didn't understand depression, and I wonder if she did. The way it pins you to the bed, can make you experience real pain, as my father did, with a coughing attack so severe he cracked a rib. How it can make you feel the world is turning against you, even the people who love you the most. How he could be two people, kowtowing one day and the next punishing me with the thick, glossy wooden ruler or throwing punches at the wall, leaving a hole beside your head.

Because of my father's "allergies" I couldn't use perfume, deodorant, hairspray, lotion, bubble bath, soap; no gerbil, no hamster, no guinea pig, no dog, no cat. Back then, if I closed my eyes a flash would pop, as if for a moment illuminating meaning. Back then the world was black and white. I thought my father lacked fortitude.

Now the lens is hazier, as if coated with Vaseline, blurred edges open to interpretation.

I used to visit an elderly neighbour after gymnastics practice; cross-legged in her living room, we'd play cards. She'd make me tea. For Christmas she gave me a bottle of toilet water and a powder puff. Now and then I'd take them out of my closet to inhale what I could of their lemony fragrance through the plastic wrap.

I was *good* at gymnastics. Within the year I was competing.

Riding home on the bus with my thrift-store bodysuit packed into the bag at my feet, I'd feel something close to integrity. I'd say to myself "I am a gymnast" and enjoy the wholeness that came with the words.

Then, at fourteen, I broke my leg. After that it would be an ongoing struggle to watch other girls my age competing at the international level. I saw in them *who I could have been.*

I hid the injury from my parents that evening, full of shame. The next morning, knowing full well the look of disappointment they'd give me, I told them. I was sent home from emergency on crutches, overcome by guilt, self-doubt, and self-recrimination for having caused everyone—including the doctor—all this trouble.

I'd never be a champion now.

Through acts of daring, boldness verging on brashness, I waged war on the only brand of womanhood I knew: my mother's submissive and neutered responses to my father's illness. I shoplifted, did drugs, smoked. I argued with my teachers. And I fought against, competed against, the only version of manhood I knew: my father's resigned ineffectuality as he'd shut his bedroom door and curl up in a ball with his disappointments.

The important thing was to brace yourself: to become hard, even a little bit of a bully. As if to prove my point I tied a boy to a tree at recess, and before the playground supervisors could arrive, I pulled down his pants for everyone to see. I noted with disgust, whenever my brother and I fought and he went crying to our father, that the "sissy" gene had been passed down to him like an ugly heirloom. I hated the way he was pampered, his favourite pastimes being hiding in my mother's laundry basket or riding bareback on her Electrolux. He polished his acts of affection to suit my mother's clucking and fussing; she doted on him, while my wildness pushed her away.

"He's younger than you. He needs more attention," she told me.

"I only got to be the baby for five years but he gets to be the baby forever," I pointed out, in what I thought was my quite clever grasp of this travesty.

She shrugged and sighed.

Like any child who, feeling neglected or abandoned, says "If I were dead, then they'd see," I played with reckless disregard for my safety. I jumped out of trees, carefree at the moment of greatest danger, exhilarated at the prospect of breaking my legs. I played with knives, examining my own reflection in the blades, holding them to my wrists, toying. When I'd been naughty I punished myself by inflicting small cuts on my arms, hiding them as I hid my counting rituals, my repeated touching of the curtains where their corners met, my compulsion for Jesus to know, minute by minute, every mundane thing I hadn't told anyone.

I read ten Bible chapters every night.

My jar of dead bees filled with yellow jackets, bumbles, honey bees, mud, and paper wasps. I'd pick them up from the sidewalk, cupping their black and yellow bodies like jewels in my hand until I could get home and put them in their glass museum. As the layers deepened each melted into the next, the improbably delicate feelers and gossamer wings becoming one with the pollen-encrusted legs. I'd open the lid at regular intervals to inhale the scent, which by now was growing a little rank.

I wanted to test my mettle. Force myself to enjoy the foul smell. How much could I endure? The reek of the bee jar was worse than the fish market where my parents shopped, and it was will, sheer will, that enabled me to inhale it with a dignified smile. One could get used to anything. At that age, my mettle was my victory.

When I was older I discovered that the question wasn't whether you could get used to something, but what price you had to pay.

My preconceptions about my parents equalled the size of what they didn't know about me. I'd never had to spend a lot of time studying. I talked too much. Teachers called me either brilliant or meddlesome for contradicting them in class and for roaming from desk to desk "helping" others with their work. I learned to hide parts of myself, learned the line between smart and too-smart. I let classmates copy my tests to quell their jealousy. I was expected by my father to do well in school, and my intellectual generosity gave me a tenuous popularity.

One day back when I was about ten or eleven, before breaking my leg, before the gymnastics and the paper route to pay for it, my friends and I wanted candy money. Earlier that morning we'd failed to sell some old toys, including a doll I'd played with so long her hair had fallen out. I sat fingering the doll's face, smearing the ink left behind after slashing her forehead with a red marker, thinking about how we'd tried fishing trash bins for pop bottles, checking every pay phone for change. That's when I remembered the Harlequin novels, those beautiful women. I yelled "Striptease!" at the top of my lungs, shocking my friends. Boys came running from every street, none with sidewalks but all with potholes deep enough to swim in. We put a sand bucket on the ground and the money they dropped in glinted.

I stole a bedsheet from my mother's linen cupboard, toppling the neatly folded stack with my grubby hand.

In my bedroom, I rehearsed what I was about to do.

When I went back outside the boys hooted and hollered, not at me but at the pictures their imaginations drew, inspired by *National Geographic* photos and the lingerie pages of catalogues.

We began.

"Da-da-da-da-dum," my friends sang.

They held the sheet in front of me. Silhouetted by the sun, behind my fabric wall, I began to undress. I doubted, as I peeled off my clothes, parcelling out titillation, that they could see much beyond a suggestion of skin, the innuendo of a bare shoulder, my short hair tickling the back of my neck.

I was acting the part of stripper. I couldn't yet have fathomed her ability to perform black magic, to manipulate the desire of her weak-kneed audience, but I understood the power for which I was competing. I threw my T-shirt, my cut-offs, and my halter top over the sheet.

A boy stands, bored, petulant. "What kind of show is this?"

"Sit down," I tell him.

Instead, he approaches. Peers over the sheet. "You're not naked!" he shouts. "Hey, everyone. She's not naked!"

I'd cheated or I'd been smart, depending on your point of view: I was wearing two layers of clothes.

The boys were jeering. Would they pounce? Demand a refund? I swallowed hard. The air now felt cold. The asphalt spread like an oil stain under the see-saws. I was scared and embarrassed. I stared—at the swings, the concrete elephant, the cigarette butts, the road that wound down toward us on the playground, the flat baseball diamond protected from the busy street by a steel fence— unsure of what to do.

In every situation there's something expected of you, some-thing that won't stop, like a ball bouncing down a hill that must reach rock bottom.

I decide to roll with it.

Don't think about it, I tell myself, and peel off the rest of my clothes as fast as I can, as if I didn't care.

The boys move as one animal, attacking the sheet. My friends do their best to protect me, anchoring the corners of the sheet to the ground. I'm pinned beneath it, fighting blind.

I'm in grade seven when the new girl, Brandy, transfers to my school. Impressed by her skin-tight jeans and eye makeup, I fawned over her. Rumour had it she'd been in a knife fight at her last school. I wanted that—her toughness, her confidence. I copied her style, bought Peter Pan boots and a purse with my paper-route money. I followed her to Topaz Park where we smoked on the bleachers; she bit the filter and grinned, her small blue eyes like ball bearings. I shuffled my feet in the alder leaves, pigeon feathers nestling against the seat. I knew Jesus loved me even when I sinned. I knew God forgave my smoking with Brandy because His Son had died for my right to be forgiven.

Brandy dragged deeply, then blew the smoke out through her nose. I tried to do the same but coughed until I heaved and my eyes watered.

She laughed.

We'd done this before and would do it again, many more times. I'd take her shoplifting, or I'd pinch my father's antidepressants and share them in the girls' washroom at lunchtime, washing them down with a homemade swill of coffee liqueur and red wine.

I continued to bring home straight A's and awards for academic achievement. The smoking, drinking, shoplifting part of myself that I hid from my parents also begged God's grace: I put religious tracts under windshield wipers in mall parking lots, proselytized to shoppers with brimming bags as they waited by the elevators. "Did you know that God, loves, *you*?" In contrition, I stopped eating to see how long I could survive on, say, an apple. Scored my skin with the tip of a protractor. Typed poems about corporal punishment, nuclear war, growing up on a potholed street with no trees.

I panicked if something prevented me from writing in my diary. I wrote as if bingeing and purging. I wrote as if to cocoon myself in lined sheets of loose-leaf. I wrote as if the words provided extra insurance that God would forgive my sins.

Brandy exhaled. "Here."

I took another drag and didn't cough this time.

After I smoked I'd wash my fingers with spit—my father picked up smells like a bloodhound. Later I'd learn to smoke out my bedroom window, tipping my body over the sill and my mother's bedding plants below.

———

That year, grade seven, no one came to watch me win first prize in a French public-speaking contest. The newspaper article written about me afterward mentioned that having won the provincials, I'd be going on to represent B.C. in Ottawa at a festival of the French language. It didn't mention how I stole my father's antidepressants to share among friends as we pretended to get high in the girls' washroom. "She's active in sports and a top student overall." I was a model child.

Two weeks after I shook Governor General Jeanne Sauvé's hand, summer holidays began. I was sent to the home of an aunt who worked as a nanny in Orange County, California. I shared the floor of her maid's quarters with my cousin, or if my aunt's job required her to attend to other things, she'd leave me in the home of refugee friends. In this home children relaxed like Peter Pan's clan of Lost Boys, spreading out on couches in front of a TV that was left on all night long. These friends owned a Vietnamese nightclub. There I'd wash and iron tablecloths with the others; we were all between twelve and eighteen. Two of us would work the door, collecting cover charges in a tiny cubicle that filled with cigarette smoke so that by the end of the night our eyes were watering. Other times the bunch of us would pile into a car and head to the pool. I called my parents and asked them to extend my flight date. This was my first taste of freedom. In this atmosphere of benign neglect, among these young Vietnamese refugees, a long-awaited sense of belonging filled me. It brought with it pride, and the feeling that I'd found home.

———

Every Saturday, in a playroom of the Queen Alexandra hospital where I volunteered, I'd sit in the lap of a Vietnamese man my father's age and admire his straight white teeth. He liked me because I was half Vietnamese, and would ask me questions about my family. He even came to our house and joked with my father, having somehow broken through his boundaries.

One Saturday my father told me I wouldn't be seeing him anymore: he was in jail. The man had been at the pool in a bathing suit and had hugged some children—he'd done nothing wrong, my father said; it had been a cultural misunderstanding. I believed him until the day he told me about an uncle of his who, while still a boy, had become a "hustler" to feed his family. They had been abandoned by his grandfather. The boy would meet men at the train station where he sold peanuts. One day, on his return home, the baby was crying but they had no food to give him, so he inserted his penis into the baby's mouth. My father told this tale in a tone of admiration. "So the baby had something to suckle on."

I wrinkled up my face. "Ew. Why didn't he just use his finger?"

My father looked at me as if I'd utterly missed the point.

At the age of twelve I published a limerick about male pattern baldness in an anthology of elementary-school verse. I wrote short stories about doomed love affairs, the Vietnam War, heroic rescues. "She's meeting boys at the library," my father would joke, when in truth I was finding vast landscapes to lose myself in, characters that kept frustration at bay. I met Tolstoy and Dostoyevsky. Still, for every Russian classic I'd read ten Silhouette romances. I chose titles according to the colour of their spines, how they jumped from the shelves. I fed on frontier fiction, prison stories, anything involving narrow escapes. Sometimes I sat on the carpet of the children's section and buried my nose in the pages, inhaling the printed word.

If my mother had noticed my jar of decomposing bees, I'd have lied and told her I was making poison. Like that time I left some bread to mould, then swallowed the rot. Now when I opened the jar the death smell made me gag. I kept inhaling. Why? Because I could.

I could take it. I could even pee into the jar, saturating their gossamer wings, and set it back on my windowsill.

Road to the Spring

When I was fourteen I had one solitary tape that I'd listen to before bed with a Walkman one of the California kids had given me. I wanted more rock 'n' roll. But fundamentalist Pentecostal beliefs forbade this—the beat could conjure demons—so I hid my growing love from my parents and from God himself by ducking under the covers and keeping the volume low. After a while, when I knew I wouldn't be happy with one tape, I went to the local department store where they had a music section in the basement. I was poring over the rows of tapes when a hand tapped my shoulder. I looked up. No one was there. I returned to examining the tapes but couldn't get rid of my shivers. Bang. It hit me. That had been the Hand of God. I started sweating. I was sinning. This was heresy. And He'd caught me out.

Yet I couldn't pull myself away from the music. If God was

against listening to the Beatles, then I was against God. Nothing that felt so good could be so bad.

That night I listened to "Helter Skelter" over and over. My Pentecostal comic books had said the devil would use the beat to possess me, and I danced as if possessed. If this was how it felt to be inspired, then I was the devil's child. Scarier was the thought that the devil, and God, didn't exist. The Bible was a story well told, and as such, capable of making the fantastical sound real.

With the speed of a bubble popping in mid-air, I was like anyone else. Cast adrift with no compass for orientation.

I could do anything I wanted.

By the age of fourteen, many of my parents' conditions had grown unbearable. My first round of counselling occurred after I rebelled against, what were to me, their ridiculous rules. I no longer hid my acts of treason. I got drunk and didn't come home. I skipped school, shrugged off the suspensions. Either the school or a friend's parents had notified the Ministry of Child and Family Development, and I'd been deemed "a child at risk." They arranged for a family therapist to counsel my parents and me in the hope of reconciliation.

The counsellor assigned to us through Child Services agreed that a sundown curfew in the wintertime, for one, was unreasonable.

I told her I wanted to be able to go out and make friends. "But how can I do that when I have to be home by five?" I told her I envied other girls' freedom to be *normal*. Whereas for me, "to see shows, to go to parties or out on a date, there always has to be a plan. Something specific, and even then I have to write a list of pros and cons that I have to hand in, like at school."

She looked at my parents in an "I'm not judging you" way, but I could tell that look hit a nerve and made them angry. The counsellor waited for a response. Riding on buses late at night, they said finally, was dangerous.

"So what about driving her?"

My mother harrumphed. My father's stony silence was all the proof I needed: nothing was going to change. That an outsider would expect them to alter their rules was, for them, deeply offensive.

My parakeet escaped the same year I did, 1986, the summer I straddled childhood and the streets, the summer I was fourteen. It had always tried the cage door with its beak, and if I hadn't locked it with a twist-tie it would flip it up and scoot out before the door slammed shut on its head. This time, though, it flew right out from its cage and into the crabapple tree in the park across the street.

My junior high was twice as large as my elementary school had been, with hundreds of students I'd never met, rows of lockers, and a different classroom for each subject.

The summer before I flew away, my parents had allowed me to visit a friend on the mainland. This display of indulgence was uncharacteristic. Did they see our proposed visit to the 1986 Vancouver Exposition as a once-in-a-lifetime learning experience? My friend's father was a doctor, and he was of German heritage and owned a mansion in one of Vancouver's priciest neighbourhoods— did their wealth awaken a hope that our family would climb the social ladder? Or were they meeting my need for independence halfway, as if to say, "You may have your freedom, but only *if* you choose the right friends."

A few years older than me, my friend worked as a bosun's mate on a schooner that sailed as an ocean-based summer camp. I'd sailed on it too, northward from Victoria to Desolation Sound then through the Georgia Strait and back to Victoria. The token brown kid there on a scholarship, the poor kid among rich preppies who'd flown in from cities across Canada.

Despite our differences, he liked me. I loved visiting him on the boat, loved the view from the bowsprit and the crow's nest. I loved sea charts and the smell of Brasso and the perfume of tar melting between the boards of the deck. And I loved the words *bulkhead*, *stanchion*, *halyard*, *fo'c'sle*. I loved that he could read the wind, sail by dead reckoning. I loved that he knew where he was going. I loved his sense of direction as much as I loved that he owned his own sailboat. Soon he was much more than a friend.

The birdcage had been placed on the cement slab of our porch, where my mother's sunflowers grew next to her lavender plants. When my bird had managed to lift the latch he must have been startled to find himself outside, among power lines and chain-link fences, barking dogs, and prowling cats. He'd flown away and I did too, a few weeks after I discovered that my boyfriend had cheated on me with someone who'd spent ten days on his boat.

A few months after my fifteenth birthday, I wrote a note in ball-point pen saying not to worry and left it on my bed. My schoolmate Luna was throwing a party and I'd been seized by the unassailable conviction that something good, something right, awaited me there. My parents wouldn't have let me go, yet somehow I knew that everything hinged on that party. My destiny had come to rest on it. I took a last look at my room and walked out—away from my home, my life, the olive carpet that clashed with my sky-blue walls. I walked away, saying under my breath, "If you can't look after me properly, I'll do it myself," full of bravado, tired of poverty. I thought about God's thwarted plan for me: I'd never be a gymnastics champion, a realization that had pierced me with an urgency more acute than the pain of my broken leg. But since then a deeper psychic pain had taken over. I would die if I stayed. I was sure of it. If I remained strapped to what felt like a time bomb, ticking away while someone out there was living the life that was supposed to be mine, I'd never grow up.

Many children grow up unloved, but they don't go to the extremes I did. Maybe this is a story about how borderline personality disorder—a diagnosis I received two years ago—develops in a child. Or maybe it's about a good girl who makes bad choices. Or maybe it's about the power we have to rationalize our worst behaviours.

I'm still trying to understand whether it was something as inborn as the colour of my eyes that made me trade a life at home for the streets. Or an obsessive need for approval generated by an inability to impress my parents. Whatever it was, I ran away from home at the age of fifteen armed with misguided convictions that allowed me to justify my recklessness, impulsivity, and promiscuity to myself. I was motivated to stay on the streets as long as I did by the firm belief that love involved self-sacrifice, that it constituted a form of noble suffering. But no one story can paint the whole picture. Love had to be earned, and you had to pay dearly to get it. That's what my life so far had taught me.

Missing persons still fascinate me. People who disappear, never to be heard from again. Holiday snapshots on the news. An old high school photo on street poles. Teary-eyed relatives begging for a safe return, asking for the public's help. Have you seen this woman, man, child? But what about those who go missing on purpose? Not taken by serial killers or kidnappers, but losing part of themselves by choice?

They think of running away every day, and the hundredth time they think it they take a step, compelled or propelled, farther than they ever thought possible.

For something to be lost, someone must be searching for it. What goes missing unmissed is not missing.

Living in the Gaps of the World

Luna was in the same junior high enrichment program as me. Her parents burned incense, ate sandwiches for dinner, and smoked hash, which they thought they'd hidden well in a Kashmir box on the bookshelf. Old hippies who used words like "emotions" and "interpersonal relationships." After Luna's party, where I'd gotten so drunk I vomited fourteen times out the front window on a canoe stored below it in the grass, I nursed my hangover with cartons of milk and figured out what to do. Luna invited me to stay with her, assuring me that her parents wouldn't mind. Luna's parents agreed that I could live with them.

On weekends Luna and I would crank AC/DC on the ghetto blaster, sing along to "Back in Black" using her mascara wand as a microphone. The days she hung out with her boyfriend I'd play with her little sister, chasing her around the living room as she skidded in footed pyjamas.

We hitchhiked, went to parties, drank Southern Comfort, met boys. We broke the law, but in small ways. At night we shared her waterbed, our arms draped around each other. In the morning we went to class and kept our grades up, on track to a good university.

My parents didn't look for me. I phoned to let them know where I was, that I was safe, but they didn't drive to Luna's house. They didn't force me into the car to return home. Unbeknownst to me, they were about to sign my custody away to the state.

Twenty years later, I accessed my family court files through the Freedom of Information Act and read what the social worker had written about me: "Suko's parents are unwilling to have her home until she has shown she can stabilize her behaviour. The parents felt Yasuko's behaviour would have a detrimental effect on their youngest child David age 10."

My parents refused to meet with the psychologist, so I continued attending sessions with him on my own. Six weeks into my stay at Luna's, which I hoped would last forever, her mother sat me down in Luna's bedroom. "You need to try and *reconcile* things with your parents," she said.

My bubble burst. They liked me, but they weren't going to adopt me. I loved it at Luna's—how we shared the same bed and each other's clothes like sisters who need no permission to borrow what they please.

I stared out into the yard, where the stillness of rhododendron leaves absorbed the raindrops' slick green migration, and considered my next move.

———

I was living in a friend's closet; he joked that he'd charge me rent. His parents worked the night shift, leaving him and his two brothers on their own, so he had no reason to keep me there. He said it was "just in case." In case his parents came home, in case any number of other things. To me it seemed outlandish. A twisted power trip. But on rainy nights when no other school friend was allowed a "sleepover party," the closet was more of a home than a park bench would have been. At least it was dry, at least it was warm.

Then I moved in with Pat. He lived in a bachelor suite close to Luna's house and sold dime bags that we bought after school. Another dealer sold cheaper joints and we pooled our change to buy two or three at a dollar apiece to share at the end of the football field by the gas station, or we smoked them in the rain at the college campus across the street from our high school under the inefficient cover of chestnut trees. Mostly we bought from Pat because he gave us a place to get high.

Pat's apartment was brown and smelled like an ashtray—he and his brother would butt their smokes in the dirty dishes scattered over the Salvation Army furniture. But the space was ours for as long as we wanted to chill there.

Pat and his brother wore ball caps and mackinaws, had money for booze but ate canned food from the tin, and seemed to have no job other than selling weed. I couldn't understand a word Pat said when we first met. He had a cleft lip and missing teeth. The bottom half of his face looked caved in, as if he'd had cancer. He hid the deformity under a full moustache and beard. My ear tuned into his garbled words as if to a foreign accent.

47

His nose barely held his thick glasses in place; he wore jeans with stains. It surprised me to learn he had a kid, a little boy, which meant, I guessed, a wife, or an ex-wife, or at least an ex-girlfriend who had custody.

Who'd sleep with *him*? I thought. But it didn't take me long to learn that a person will sleep with another for many reasons, and it's not always as simple as love or desire.

Pat had been *a good guy*, letting me hang out, and sometimes after school Luna would drop by. Lansdowne Junior Secondary didn't want me. I scarcely showed up to class, and when I did I lacked interest, sometimes even falling asleep at my desk. But when Luna would visit it felt like old times. We talked about how my parents refused to attend any more therapy sessions, how I'd paid for my own gymnastics classes while my brother received equestrian gear and riding lessons, how I played alone while my mother would sit with my brother among the trains and cars that looped around an elaborate village they'd made with lights and tiny people.

"Forget about it," Luna would say.

That December, the principal called me into his office. I sat in a grey chair under a grey ceiling. His sporty haircut made him look like a soccer coach. He had pictures on his desk of his family, which he kept glancing at as he talked. "We think an alternative program would be better suited to your needs. Your disciplinary problems, your last suspension . . ."

Alternative school? I felt insulted. I was still on the honour roll. "Whatever," I said, and sank down into my seat.

No matter which way I turned my head I couldn't escape either the grey or the glare that shone down from his fluorescent lights.

They buzzed while I thought of the implications. People who went to alternative schools were dumb, needed extra help, couldn't hack it in regular classes. Pregnant girls attended alternative programs, or bullies, or those who broke into tears at the first sign of difficulty with an assignment. Trigonometry? Forget it. Instead there'd be sculpting things from clay, learning how to maintain personal hygiene. Teachers talking in soft voices.

"Good grades or not . . ." he said, trailing off. I'd screwed up my end of the bargain. His voice had the apologetic tone of a breakup. "It's not you, it's me."

They could expel me from Lansdowne, but there'd be no touchy-feely curriculum replacing it. No matter what my parents thought, or the school principal, or society, I wanted the life out there that belonged to me. "Go out and find it," I whispered to myself. "Take what's yours."

Now I was at Pat's and drunk-dialing an ex-boyfriend's phone number while Luna chugged the last drops of my Malibu. My fingers moved through a boozy haze as I dropped the phone, picked it up again, and succeeded in punching in the right digits.

"Steve? Hello? Are you there?"

Luna pried the phone out of my hand. "I'm sorry, Steve, she's really wasted," she said.

I lunged for the phone. "Steve, I love you. I really, really love you."

Luna yanked the phone away. "She says she loves you but she can't come see you tonight." She hung up.

I started bawling.

"You don't look good."

I ran to the bathroom. I puked into the toilet. Then I blacked out.

At some point I became aware that Pat's brother had popped his head into the washroom. "Are you okay?"

I nodded, gripping the toilet seat.

He hoisted me to my feet and, standing behind me, gathered my hair so I wouldn't vomit on it. "That's it, that's it, let it all out."

As I heaved into the dirty toilet, he ground his body into mine . . .

He was unbuttoning my jeans, then he'd taken his pants off. His words, "That's it, baby," ended when I turned, pushed him away, and stumbled over a river of dirty clothes and empty beer cans to the living room.

The Hide-A-Bed reeked of smoke and sweat. I must have fallen asleep. I wasn't aware of time passing, dawn breaking, until I woke up with Pat's hands under the blankets, cold as permafrost, reaching between my legs.

"Jesus fuck, Pat!" I sat up. "What are you doing?"

"Nothing," he said.

"Don't do that."

"Okay. I'm sorry."

"Geez, what are you, a fuckin' perv?"

I went back to sleep, but awoke a few minutes later with Pat on top of me.

I was sober enough now to grab my duffle bag, its weight pulling my arm to the floor. "I'm fuckin' outta here," I said. But that's when I realized I'd lost the rest of my clothes. I was wearing a tank top, and rain battered the window.

Where would I go anyway?

I returned to bed, fighting against every instinct I had to lie back down on the flipped-open, pulled-out thing that stank, that reminded me too much of my old living room chair as a child. I lay there rigid, exerting the effort of an athlete to remain still, biding my time until the rain stopped, until the buses started running, until I could walk out not with shame but with pride, until the new replaced the old in my body. *I was never coming back.* Comforting myself with the word *never*. With the "Now they'll see. Now they'll be sorry" of my childhood. Every nerve ending was on edge, poised for battle.

If I stayed still long enough, could I disappear?

When morning came, and the first sound of buses, I found my clothes. Rain was still falling.

For the next few weeks I slept in bandstands, bus stops, and stairwells, using my clothes as a pillow. The streets were always the noisiest when the bars let out, then they'd quiet again. The coldest time of night was never its middle but right before dawn, a last push to freeze anyone still outside. Each stairwell I slept in I'd make homey with whatever I could find, ordering my cigarette butts, naming the pigeons and appropriating them as pets, shifting this bit of garbage from one corner to the other. By moving something within it I made each space mine, at least for an hour or two until security would tell me to "move on."

One night I snuck into the Empress Hotel, a national historic site and the costliest place in town, and crashed in the basement next to the vacuum cleaners. I hitchhiked, asking, "Where's the party?" I learned how to absorb my menstrual flow with the ripped-off corner of a kitchen sponge, rinsing it in the toilets of public bathrooms before reinserting it. I hardened myself. No shame in survival. There was no disgust, only satisfaction in doing what needed to be done.

To survive, swing your arms, keep your hands out of your pockets unless they're wrapped around a switchblade. Learn how long to hold a stare to prove you're not intimidated. My needs had been reduced to dry clothes, food, and a place to sleep, in that order. I schlepped two tote bags around, going to the food fairs in malls and asking people, "Are you going to finish that?"

Freedom came with hardship. I reminded myself, Isn't this what you wanted?

In the months to come, I panhandled. The coins in my pocket jangled; cupping their solidity in my hand calmed me. Then I refined my straightforward panhandle into a hustle. One involved stationing myself in front of bars at two in the morning.

"Mister, I'm so sorry to bug you," I'd say to men who were not drunk and with a woman. "I missed my bus. My stepdad, he's such an asshole. There's no way I'm going to make it home in time." Then I'd cry, "Oh my god, I don't know what to do. My friends were drinking. I didn't want to go with them. Oh shit, oh shit. The last time I was late my stepdad beat me. Oh shit."

No man wanted to look like a schmuck in front of his girlfriend, so he'd drag out his wallet and relinquish a twenty-dollar bill.

If I began to feel down, I'd turn to poetry to lift my spirits.

Underworld Prison and Chamber of Ice

Carey Road was a receiving home, a cross between a group home and a halfway house, a splint for troubled youth. After therapy failed to reunite me with my family, the system had forced me there. But I could lie still until morning, pretend to be sleeping, bide my time.

On my first day I went into the pinball room where a boy with a shaved head played, a cigarette hanging out of his mouth.

"Got an extra smoke?" I asked.

He scowled. "No, I don't have an *extra* smoke."

I shot him a look, then stepped closer—you don't intimidate me—and glanced over his shoulder to see his score. Before I knew it he'd pushed me, sending me flying off my feet backward. "Fuck off!" he yelled.

Welcome to Carey Road.

An office by the front door was the only thing that made the house look institutional. It was impossible to explain to the counsellors who lived and worked there that the ideology of the streets made the wood floors and sparse furnishings of Carey Road no more than a badly decorated waiting room on our way to freedom— the freedom to go hungry, the freedom to piss on a street corner, the freedom to beg leftovers from the malls' food fairs.

One evening after dinner, about two weeks into my stay, a girl named Ruth and I caught a bus downtown to the Thunderbird Motel. She was a seventeen-year-old prostitute who lived across the hall from me. "Be careful," the youth worker had warned me. "Ruth has . . . *problems*."

Ruth's boyfriend had a room at the Thunderbird that he shared with another man. A shitty motel across the street from the park. The kind of place that should have been full of overseas tourists but was full of people who looked like us, hitting town to buy or sell anything from hot stereos to heroin. The room had two beds and a kitchenette. Knives blackened from smoking hash littered the stovetop.

Away from Carey Road, anything could happen. I sat on the edge of my seat, as firm as a hand, waiting for it, watching Ruth's boyfriend tie her off with a belt that had silver stars on it. I liked to observe Ruth's pupils contract to points when he plunged the needle of Dilaudid into the crook of her arm. While Ruth shot up I sat with her boyfriend's roommate; he was shirtless at the Formica table, a can of beer in front of him. He had lips I could imagine kissing, satin hair that hung to his shoulders. I drank one cherry vodka cooler after another. I'd already decided the moment I saw him that if he wanted to fuck me, I was ready. I wanted real sex, with someone who was beautiful, who mattered. My encounter with the act at Pat's hadn't counted. If you hadn't asked for it, it never happened. Even the twelve-year-old girl down the hall at Carey Road had a boyfriend. It was time for me to have one, too.

Drunk, high, all four of us got on a bus headed for Carey Road, and from our seats at the back we laughed at the top of our lungs, making passengers glare in our direction. Once at the receiving home we tiptoed through the shadows cast by the oak trees that lined the driveway. Then, after showing the two men the fire-escape stairs to the bathroom window, Ruth and I strode through the front door, checked in with our workers, and went upstairs to let them in.

We all went to Ruth's room. My boyfriend-to-be and I flopped down on her extra bed and slipped under the covers still wearing our clothes. The beds were side by side, a few feet apart. My toes tangled in the bedsheet as I wriggled closer to him so that I could undo the button fly of his jeans, yank his T-shirt away from his belt. I traced his contours: his chest, his nipples, his jutting ribs. Then slid my hand lower, finding a thick, rigid cock. The scent of his deodorant mixed with Ruth's perfume intoxicated me.

The thrill of Ruth's bad-girlness had brought me into the bedroom with her as much as my desire for true love, to have it inside me, to absorb its power. In a way my parents could never have imagined I'd become myself, defining myself against the parameters of what Ruth, her boyfriend, and his roommate needed and wanted me to be.

The warm, wet noise of her boyfriend's mouth between Ruth's legs made the heat between mine rise. The springs squeaked as he covered her body with his own, two leaves pressed together.

I watched his buttocks moving between her open legs as I undressed and brushed each piece of my clothing over the face of the man in my bed; I wanted him to smell me, need me. I fluffed my hair and lay my head on the pillow, tugged my lover toward me, my foot on the back of his knee.

Ruth moaned in her bed and I in mine. I dug my heels into the man on top of me, squirming beneath him at the sound of her short sharp breaths. We kissed. He was still wearing his underwear; where the head of his cock pressed up against me the fabric was damp, and chilly at first, but the cotton created a good-strange friction that began to dissolve me.

He ripped off his underwear. Amid a flurry of squeaking springs I felt a sharp pain, and then no pain as he entered me. My back was up against the mattress coils. Ruth moaned like a pro. I, too, moaned on cue with every thrust, thinking this is what you were supposed to do. Someone shushed us from the hall. I giggled. I thought, Finally, it's over. But unlike what I had prepared for, I felt no love. Luna and people like her had led me to believe that the act was special. I felt nothing extraordinary. Only something primitive, something universal to our animal nature. I felt predictable. Typical. Common.

In two weeks I'll pass this man on the street. We won't nod at each other. We won't even smile. We'll walk past as if we were strangers. He doesn't remember my name.

The next day I went downtown with Ruth again. One block from City Hall, on the same street as an outdoor supply shop and the locked doors of a nightclub that wouldn't open until eight p.m., in broad daylight, she swayed her hips, and smiled, and winked, and blew kisses at traffic. Then she hopped into a stranger's car, flipping her long brown hair without looking back at me. She returned twenty minutes later. I'd been worried about her the whole time, biting my nails to the quick.

We'd reached the corner of Yates and Broad when I asked her, "What do you do if . . . it doesn't work? If the man, you know, doesn't finish? Then what? Does he get mad? Do you have to give back the money?"

"No!" She laughed. "You *never* give a refund." I puzzled over her lack of fear, her smile with its immortal exuberance, her promiscuous zest.

Hell Guards

I stole things and sold them on the street for a third of their cost: butane curling irons, Black Magic chocolates, diapers, whatever people wanted me to steal. I also sold grams on Yates Street in front of the pizzeria, up the street from the Day & Night greasy spoon. I stashed my supply of dime bags and chocolate-covered mushrooms in the wall of a florist's shop on the corner.

I went AWOL from the receiving home and lived with a group of people I considered family: Johnny, Dave, and Juanita Call-Me-Chris. Some nights we prowled the streets, keeping our legs in motion to stay warm, waiting for dawn's rays before sleeping outside. When we could afford it, we slept in motels that had sprouted fungus-like between gas stations and blue-collar apartment towers in the Burnside Gorge neighbourhood. I remember everything.

I can tell you which motels have beds that are cleaner than others, which ones have a saggy mattress that your body falls into. Some have a Magic Fingers box on the night stand that costs a quarter: I've always wanted to try but can't justify spending twenty-five cents for a massage. I know everything about these motels, their floral bedspreads, their nubby bedspreads, which ones have bedspreads that are stiff, or soft, or itchy. The fingerprints in the grime on the laminate headboard, the table lamps and the locker-room smell of the carpet. How a cigarette burn feels like a scar when you run your hand over a table scorched with them. I can tell you where the pop machines are and where to find ice. I can tell you about chain locks and spoons burned black, rips in vinyl chairs, and which proprietor will trade a room for sex. Dusty glass protects yellowing prints of mountains or moose or dappled streams or flower bouquets in brass-coloured frames. Some rooms have curtains. Some curtains are too threadbare to darken a room. Some rooms have bottle openers built into the fake wood panelling and others are decorated with torn wallpaper. I know them all. People have cooked rocks in this room. Shot up in this room. Been beaten here. I know the shapes of the stains on their bathroom floors, I know which rooms you need to be eighteen to rent, which one is carpeted with Astroturf, which one's key has a red plastic tag. The Friendship Inn, the Sherwood Park, the Jolly Knight, the Scotsman, the Coachman, the Robin Hood, the Oxford, the Dutchman, the Doric, the Traveller's Inn, the Tally-Ho, the Colonial. I know them all.

Since we earned less than three dollars on each gram of weed, we couldn't always afford a motel. We'd wash in gas station bathrooms, have Cheezies for breakfast, and when my tank tops got too dirty to wear as shirts I'd wear them as miniskirts, the dirt being further down and so less noticeable. I learned how to turn a T-shirt back to front, then inside out, and wear it three times longer. I convinced myself it was romantic. We were no different from nomads seeking their own desert oasis. Shunned by society. Outcasts. We were hunting for paradise. We were a new breed of pioneer, our untamed wilderness the urban jungle.

Yvonne, a well-known working girl, always had a motel room, wore a rabbit fur coat, and, at twenty-five, walked like someone who knew exactly where she was going, like someone unafraid.

She lived with her boyfriend at the Skyline Motel, a five-minute cab ride from where I sold drugs. She felt sorry for me, or she thought I had potential, or she saw my vulnerability. My need for love made me exploitable; I wore my weakness like an open wound. She took me under her wing. I'd watch her put on lipstick in the afternoons, chin in my hands, gazing with the love of a child who hopes to one day be as beautiful as her mother.

Yvonne could cuss out anyone, but she made it sound like poetry: she'd picked up her verbal-assaults-turned-fine-art from her Jamaican boyfriend, Nicky, who, with his waist-length dread-locks, also never ceased to astonish and thrill me. That a couple like them had taken an interest in me made me feel special. I worried that I'd say something stupid when Yvonne curled her eyelashes or slid her feet into six-inch heels; she'd notice the look in my eye and say, "Girl, what's wrong with you?" I already knew she thought my crush on Johnny, one of my roommates—his blue eyes, his Bon Jovi hair—was moronic. I basked in his presence despite his basic disregard of mine, even on nights we shared a motel room and a bed. The truth was I'd "chosen" this street family because Johnny was in it. The possibility of romance overrode Yvonne's assertions that he was a waste of my time. Every day she told me I should *grow up*. But there was no way to tell Yvonne that once upon a time, when Johnny was drunk, he'd kissed me, and that I'd do anything short of murder to have his tongue in my mouth again.

Once, when Yvonne and I were in Harvey's, where she'd bought me a burger because she knew I hadn't eaten in days, she asked me, "What's he going to do for you?"

I wished I had an answer. He was unemployed and of no fixed address. All he had was an Ibanez guitar, an Adidas bag full of dirty clothes, and a father who wanted him to work in forestry. But the way he *played* his guitar turned my heart into water. As did the way he could throw a roundhouse kick, his foot connecting with a solid *thwap* against anyone's head.

But I was only fifteen and Johnny was nineteen, and fifteen was Johnny not talking to me as a woman. Fifteen could never be as beautiful as twenty-two; fifteen was jailbait. Pimply boys my own age riding BMXs, fat men with beards and leather vests who wagged their tongues between their fingers and said "I eat great pussy"— they wanted me. Not Johnny. If I'd answered Yvonne's question with "He's going to love me," she would have laughed. And if I'd told her the truth, that "It's not what he's going to do for me but what I'm going to do for him," she'd stop grooming me. Then *poof*, no more Yvonne to show me the ropes.

Today Yvonne was in bed, ringed by Kleenex, but she was still taking me downtown. Her grit was inspiring. Coughing and feverish one second, her nose red and sore, the next she was putting on makeup to hide the blotches on her face. I'd taken a shower and my hair was clean. I'd put on a fresh set of clothes. Yvonne had started blow-drying my hair when she ducked into the bathroom, looking for something she'd forgotten.

"Suko," she said. Something about her tone put me on edge.

She stood in the doorway, pointing down. Had I left a mess? My clothes in a heap on the floor? I rose and walked sheepishly toward what she was pointing at. A large puddle of water leaking beneath the metal transition strip and beginning to soak the motel room's carpet.

She led me to the shower curtain. "You have to put this," she said, grabbing it, "on the inside of the tub. *This* is where it belongs."

I hung my head. Why was I such an idiot? Had dope fogged my brain? A lack of food and sleep? My parents didn't have a curtain but a shower door; still, that couldn't explain it. Yet I remember the water, Yvonne's look of dismay, and my shame. I waited for her to yell. I waited for her to slap me.

She smiled, her frown giving way to a smile that showed the gap between her front teeth that I'd always thought was one of the prettiest things about her.

Yvonne and I could have walked to the shoe store, but instead we caught a cab. Downtown, in the middle of the day, bustled with people. I sat up straighter, lifting my chin to look down my nose at them the way Yvonne did.

She talked about the places we would visit together, across Canada. "But I'll make you go back to school. You can study by correspondence," she said. "A good education is really important."

I raised my eyebrows. She looked me square in the eye and told me that she worked to pay for her son's boarding school. I'd heard of this school, a prestigious one up-island.

She had everything together. She had it all. A bright motel room, hair-styling implements, a boxful of makeup, respectable clothing, a modern haircut, a boyfriend, the walk, the talk, a reputation on the street. To badmouth her spelled swift and severe retaliation. Yvonne had everything anyone could ever want. She ate and shopped where she liked. Had money to burn. The world she'd surrounded herself with radiated and reflected her talents, her smile, its undercurrent of danger, her hospitality bestowed on the few and deserving. She controlled this world. She decided who entered or left. Things didn't happen to her; she made things happen.

Each day as I grew to know her, I liked her more. She still scared me, but I appreciated my fear—if you played with a black panther, you accepted its ferocity as part of the intrigue and challenge of the game. Under her influence I could become someone to be proud of, someone like her. A person people smiled at because they dared *not* smile.

I wasn't surprised she had a son in boarding school. I could picture his uniform, his curly hair and dark skin, a rare addition among the all-white offspring of the rich—blond boys who went sailing in the summer and snowboarding in the winter. A school-aged son at twenty-five would have meant a teen pregnancy. I was reminded of a friend who'd gotten pregnant in grade nine or ten. Remembered her at eight months along, sitting in the dark kitchen of her mother's house, waiting for her boyfriend to visit. She was fat, dressed in track pants, her greasy hair hanging down. She didn't look happy. Her face didn't even look like the same face I'd gone to school with, partied with, shared beer and tokes with. I felt sorry for her. But the news of Yvonne's son made me realize that anything was possible. If I followed the right path, my "possible" would turn from the enforced domesticity of a drab kitchen to being able to buy my way into a boarding school, or beyond.

Prostitutes were not known for being responsible or successful. Yet for the first time I realized how society could be wrong. How people could claim a certain knowledge while misjudging a situation. I became suspicious: what else had society lied about? What else had I been persuaded to believe?

The world had turned upside down. Everything bad was good and everything good had become pompous, hyperinflated with the air of its own self-righteousness.

Did she really have a son? Or had she invented him to make herself appear "safer," to convince me of how much money I could make if I followed in her footsteps to the track?

The boarding school was an hour and a half away, meaning she wouldn't see him except on holidays. But if she was working the streets to send him there it would mean something that every parent knows: there is nothing they won't do for their child. No vile place they won't plunge into to make for them a perfect world.

To get a job, any job—as my father had, in a foreign country— ranked as a success. At the time I didn't recognize this. Only that Yvonne had makeup, clothes, a son in boarding school.

Still trying to reconcile what I knew of the streets with this unexpected attitude of someone in them, I listened to the picture she described, putting me in the centre of it, in a train car, textbooks spread over the little table, leaning over them in a silk blouse, every piece of my tasteful luggage in the bin overhead.

She took what she wanted from life, this woman. I thought of Johnny's respect, reverence, when he sold her a joint. I wanted him to treat me that way, wanted him to see me the way he saw Yvonne. I wanted to have that power. I wanted to have that control.

———

In the shoe store, Yvonne chose a pair of orange stilettos for me. "These will look great with your shirt."

I turned them over to see the price tag glued to the bottom. "You got to be kidding me."

She took them to the till.

I couldn't stop her. The next thing I knew the clerk was ringing them in.

Yvonne pulled something out of her wallet I'd never seen before: a bill the colour of arterial blood. On the back was a ring of horses, each with a rider wearing a jacket the same colour.

Yvonne held the fifty in the palm of her hand. "Don't worry," she said. "You'll be seeing a lot more of these." Then she winked at me.

Torture by Mincing Machines

Empathy isn't the same as *being* someone else. My sense of separateness was mirrored by the sunshine that could never inhabit the motes it lit up in Yvonne's hotel room. Those motes would never be able to curl themselves around that warmth, to become it; as soon as they tried it would disappear. In the shoe store Yvonne had reacted first with amusement and then surprise at the fact that I'd never seen a fifty-dollar bill up close. Now I was strutting in front of a jewellery shop on the corner of Broad and View. I'd thought, Maybe if I make some real money Johnny will respect me enough to want his tongue in my mouth.

Juanita Call-Me-Chris would go with me for safety. We ducked into a doorway out of the wind. I wobbled in the red boots I'd borrowed from Yvonne, soft as butter, a size too big, the heels higher than any I'd yet worn.

I watched the cars roll past. Then a man pulled over, asked if I was working. Chris and I had discussed this; we'd planned. But the first words out of my mouth were "Fuck off, you sick prick."

He cocked his head, confused. As he turned to pull away I felt an urgency; I flashed to Johnny's lips, the way I'd kiss him, and thought, What the hell am I doing?

"Yes," I yelled. "Yes, I'm working."

We drove to his house, me in the front seat of his little green car, Chris in the back. I looked for her eyes in the rear-view but she was staring out the window, avoiding my gaze.

As if to allay the moral misgivings that had made me swear at him, the man pointed at girls our age lounging at bus stops in tight jeans, swinging their ankles in lazy circles or digging for lip gloss in their tote bags. "Every girl," he said, "do a little something." I wasn't sure if I believed him, but it didn't matter.

At the man's house he showed Chris the living room—heavy curtains and floral-patterned couch—and told her to make herself at home. Then he gave her a bottle of homemade wine, told her we wouldn't be long, and led me to the bedroom. It was tidy, with a crocheted blanket over the mattress.

What did I think about as I turned my first trick? Johnny. How proud he'd be.

When we were done the man paid me with a fifty-dollar bill. As beautiful and red and ringed with horses as Yvonne's had been. Now I'd be able to support my street family. Johnny and I would end up a real couple, like Yvonne and Nicky.

———

"We can get a motel room," I said.

Johnny stood on the corner of Broad and Yates and looked at the money in my hand. He retrieved his stash from an alcove and turned. "Well?" he said. "What are you waiting for?"

I grabbed the others and flagged a cab. Johnny gave me a strange kind of grin. With my family in the taxi—Chris by my side, Dave in front—we drove toward the Gorge and then pulled into a gas station where I bought a carton of Neapolitan ice cream. I paid the clerk with the fifty. I luxuriated as he counted out my change.

Back in the taxi, I talked a mile a minute about how I could even buy Johnny the newest Ibanez he'd drooled over in the last issue of *Guitar Player* magazine.

Dave was the oldest at twenty-one. We sent him in to pay for the room and waited by the ice machines. After looking both ways and scooting through the parking lot, we were inside. Dave threw the keys on top of the television; they clinked with authority. Then he disappeared into the washroom to take a shower. Chris fell asleep the instant her head hit the pillow.

Johnny and I were on the bed. Here was the moment I'd been waiting for.

"You know," he said, "now you're nothing but a fucking hooker."

I crumbled inside. But I wouldn't let him see me cry. I'd suck things up. And no matter how broken I felt, no one would ever know how much he'd let me down.

Dave emerged from the washroom, releasing a cloud of steam into the room. I hurried past him with my ice cream and locked the door behind me. I cried perched on the toilet seat, scooping the Neapolitan from the carton, managing two small mouthfuls. Then I ran a bath, and in an act of defiance no one saw, left the carton in the sink to melt. As if proving I didn't care at all.

———

I'd been commissioned by a friend who bought drugs from me to steal a pair of acid-wash jeans, and though I hardly boosted anymore, I thought of this job as a personal favour. Jeans could be tricky: you had to dig through stacked shelves to find a specific size, drawing attention from clerks. Still, I had a system, an over-the-shoulder bag, and a friend to look out. Chris was blocking the manager's view, and I'd slipped the jeans under my arm when the manager strode toward us.

I ran out the door, around the corner, and halfway down the block. Chris was right next to me. Looking back, I could see the manager chasing us. I made for a stairwell but ended up at the bottom of it, trapped with nowhere to go—the clerk had somehow beaten me to it and now stood a few steps up. I had the fleeting thought that I should knock her down, run, but the moment passed. She grabbed my wrist. The next thing I knew Chris and I were following her back to the store, where I'd be charged with theft.

Now I was back in the system. As a condition of my probation I was ordered to attend school and reside where directed, which turned out to be a group home on Ashgrove Street.

The oldest girl was eighteen. Though she was friendly enough, she hardly said a word, just smiled. She lived on the ground floor next to Doreen and her husband, Kevin, our house parents. The other six of us lived two to a room. Evenings we'd sit in the basement playing video games, and days we'd go to school.

Each night, leaning on my windowsill, I'd stare at the street-lamps, trying to will myself into the light. Then, when everyone was asleep, I'd clamber out the bathroom window and crawl across the steep roof toward the fire-escape ladder, clutching my shoes in one hand and gripping the slippery shingles with the other, trying not to think about the thirty-foot fall. I'd make my way down the ladder, breathing a sigh of relief when my feet touched ground.

I worked a corner by the Empress Hotel, a few blocks from the harbour. Wind whipped my hair, the cold stung my ankles, but I was away from the group home and living, I thought, my own life. I never stayed out for more than one date and I always showed up for school the following day. Why did I do this? I know it had something to do with proving myself, or proving *to* myself—and to Johnny—that the money I earned made me strong and not "just a ho." It had something to do with free will and my own weak life. Rectifying an imbalance. Believing that my problems were manufactured by the system.

Tomorrow I'd wake up at seven, leave the group home weighted by the books in my backpack, catch two different buses to Esquimalt High. But tonight I could be anyone.

I could reinvent myself on the barren downtown streets.

One night I smiled and motioned to the lone car circling the block, its driver a year or two older than me.

He said he had fifteen dollars.

"That's it?"

I crossed my arms and drummed my fingers on my chest while I thought how the night would be wasted if I didn't have something to show for it, however paltry the sum. I agreed to give him a blow job for the five-dollar bills.

The next day I fell asleep during social studies class. When I awoke, the teacher was shaking my elbow. The others had left, the two of us remained.

He looked at me earnestly, as if he wanted to hold my hand. "Have you ever been abused?"

His words silenced me. I drew my arms across my chest, my loose white tank top with no bra, and mumbled something like "What do you mean?"

I felt transparent, defensive. Insulted by his question without knowing why. The bizarre thought occurred that he was trying to hit on me. My face reddened. I grabbed my books, stormed out with as much confidence as I could muster, and stomped off to the nurse's office. By the time I arrived my face was flushed and sweating.

She asked if I wanted to call anyone.

"No one's home," I lied. "And I'm not feeling well."

I cried myself to sleep in the comfort of the sick room until the bell rang.

Late one night I came home to find the bathroom window locked. I'd been caught. I walked away with the clothes on my back.

Abundance City

I moved into a three-bedroom house on Austin Avenue with bikers who flipped coke. They'd been friends of Johnny's, supplying him with the drugs he sold.

I had warrants. In time, the police would catch me. But I decided to live for the moment.

We pooled our money. We could afford to snort coke, to do lines or cocoa puffs instead of freebasing or banging it. We "got high on our own supply" and it didn't seem to matter. We always had enough money for breakfast at diners where the servers knew us and the cooks would laugh when one of the guys, who was handsome and funny, walked into the kitchen and spanked the women with a spatula.

We went to Thetis Lake, a twenty-minute drive from Victoria even on mornings when we'd been up all night. We always had enough cash in our pockets to buy what we needed on the half-hour drive, like beach towels or swim shorts or another cooler full of beer.

Will was the most talented of the three. He'd drawn the home-made and jailhouse tattoos that covered him.

He cooked my cocaine into rocks for me, and if he pocketed some after dropping a hit into my pipe, I'd ignore it. Share and share alike, right? After one good hit on the pipe the world disappeared, and I'd be accepted into a place of wonder and light where nothing could touch me. Where I loved everyone. Would die or kill for a stranger. After a good toke I'd be part of the connective tissue of humanity. For ten, fifteen minutes. Before needing one more. Then one more. Then one more. Always one more.

Will took no shit and dominated the household's pecking order. By allying myself with him, by straddling him in bed, pointing to each scar and having him tell me its story, by fucking him, I grew stronger. Nights we smoked crack and rolled around as naked as children until the sun came up and the birds began singing.

The year I turned sixteen, girls stood elbow to elbow like china dolls on a display shelf that stretched from the Inner Harbour to the clubs on Yates Street.

Other girls stayed out till all hours, but because I was a renegade, the word they used for a prostitute working the track without a pimp, it never occurred to me to make more money than I needed for blow, or chocolate bars, or going out to eat. I went to work and turned a trick and sometimes took myself out for dinner, which often included chiding myself. *You girl. Sit up straight. Hold up your head and don't order in your little-girl voice. You're embarrassing.*

Every night I was getting better at not speaking deferentially to the waiters, and every night the stares I drew from other customers bothered me less.

I deserved nice things. I treated myself to them. I raised myself up and stashed the money I brought home, rolled it up and hid it inside a sweater in the loft where I slept. Sometimes I counted it, slowly, before putting it back, thinking, My loft. My waterbed. My house. That house was 1930s Arts and Crafts bungalow clad in wooden shingles and a timbered porch. Much better than my parents' house. It had a profusion of windows, real stairs, a front and a back door, three bedrooms, four dogs: pit bulls, and friends. The door always open. Harleys on the green grass. We lived near the Gorge Waterway, where the curving road was lined with houses good families owned. When we'd come home from a party the pre-dawn water would shine like a dinner plate, flat and smooth.

Each morning during my first weeks on Austin Avenue I'd wake up and crank my favourite album on the stereo. A song by Boston about being forgotten by those you left behind.

One night I got high with a Coke-can crack pipe and music blaring and I sang along and remembered my parents, whom I'd seen only a few times since our unsuccessful bouts of family therapy.

Dawn dripped through tall double-hung windows onto the scarred linoleum floor. The kitchen smelled like dog. I passed Will the pipe and picked at the tuft sneaking from a rip in the vinyl kitchen chair. It occurred to me: I could take my parents out for lunch.

Between hits, I curled my hair and put on eyeshadow and lipstick and changed outfits several times. I donned a pair of classy alligator-skin shoes and a three-hundred-dollar wool coat—of which I was overbearingly proud—and called a taxi. In real life, the wool coat was two sizes too large and the hem dragged on the pavement, no longer white but filthy.

I was a teenager playing dress-up, waiting in a chair at the front window. I took another hit of crack, jerking back the curtains every time I heard a sound.

The taxi arrived at six-thirty a.m.

My parents had no idea I was coming.

I grabbed my matching alligator purse and stumbled outside into the sun.

I fiddled with my hair in the back of the cab.

My father appeared from the house as we pulled up.

I rolled down the window. "Hi, Pop!"

He stood on the other side of the fence. He made no move to open the gate.

I hesitated, my hand lingering on the cab door. I began to sweat. He stood looking at me, his lips pressed in judgment.

"Let's go for lunch," I said. "Come on, anywhere, the fanciest place." Then I added, in case it wasn't understood, "My treat."

"I don't want your money," my father said, rendering the bills I'd use to pay for lunch as dirty as the method I'd employed to earn them.

Anger replaced my crack euphoria. The balloon of pride that had swelled in my chest on the ride over burst and deflated.

"Do you know how expensive a cab is from my place?" I wasn't fishing for a contribution but underlining my success: I was someone who could afford it.

"Let me pay for the cab," my father said, missing the *how well I was doing* point. "Come in for toast."

Why shouldn't my father, along with my mother and brother, hop into the cab that instant even though it was seven in the morning and he was in his pyjamas? "Forget it."

I flipped up my collar and hopped back into the taxi I hadn't yet gotten completely out of, a gesture of shamelessness. Forget reconnection. Forget it's been such a long time. *Forget about me.*

"Hit it," I told the driver. I looked back to see my father's thin pyjamas flapping in the breeze, his figure shrinking behind the fence.

I adopted a tough-girl stance in miniskirts and five-inch heels that pinched my toes. I didn't feel like me—not the old me—and what remained was a hole full of question marks. So I set myself to becoming the best prostitute I could be.

Some tricks finished fast and some finished slow. Some talked dirty and some didn't talk at all. Some spoke in whispers and some shouted. Some brought me jewellery or other small presents. Some tried to steal their money back. Each man was different but everyone was the same, wanting to play games, to be spanked, to be diapered, to wear my underwear. They paid extra for these things. Some wanted to be coddled, some to be peed or shat on. Some wanted to shit on you. Which I wouldn't let them do. Some wanted to be tied up and some wanted to tie me up. I wouldn't let them do that either, no matter how much money they offered.

Some were fat and some were fit. Some wore shoes and some wore sneakers. The sneakers often paid better than the shoes. Some tried to pay in drugs. Some wanted to argue about the condom and some wore two or three. Sometimes I felt mad, but usually I felt nothing at all.

I never remembered their names.

———

Saturday night and some traffic throws eggs. Others throw pennies out the windows, or firecrackers, or they yell "Slut!" before speeding off.

Some men talk as if they want sex even though they don't have a dime to save their dog's life. This is what you must get good at: knowing how to distinguish those with money from those with none. How to distinguish the men who want to kill you from the ones who don't. How to dance on the line as if you were the worm in a sea of fish. Even the ones with money expect you to chase them.

The night before, an international lawyer wanted me to paint his cock with my lipstick. He signed me into his office building—one of those downtown glass towers that echoes with the silence of a cathedral—and took me up to the twenty-first floor. He didn't want sex, just someone who'd listen as he pointed his finger at his aquarium and talked about his exotic electric blue lobsters and freshwater stingrays swimming behind the glass.

Then I took out a schoolteacher. He had a whole closet full of women's clothes at his hotel room, high heels to match, and a chest full of makeup. He asked me to make him beautiful, so I did. I used blue and violet eyeshadow and purple lipstick. When he posed for me on the bed, I took Polaroid pictures of him. He asked me to call him Betty. After the photo shoot he said I should open my own house, with all the costumes in assorted sizes available for good paying customers (he'd paid me five hundred). His eyes held such excitement. "That's exactly what I'm going to do," I lied.

"Yes, baby," he said. "That's what I'm talking about."

The next man I took out was nervous, twisting his fingers. He sat in his blue jeans and jacket on the chair across the room from me, giggling, looking down and running his hands through his hair. He paid me four bills from a stack of hundreds. After he undressed, he had a nice time. Afterward, I asked him what he did for a living.

"Rob banks."

"I've never taken out a bank robber before. I bet you tip," I said. As a joke.

And he did, another fifty bucks.

I can do any one of a million things and all of them would be the truth.

A few nights later, I was leaving work. I'd flagged a cab and had shut its door when I heard a sharp knock at the window. Cat-eyed Ruth. Junkie Ruth from the receiving home. How long since I'd seen her? I sized her up, the pinpoint pupils and the way, when I rolled down the window, she pressed her body against the cab. High, drunk, or both, she slurred, "Hey, Suko."

"Hey. Ruth."

"You going in?" She nodded toward the doorway of Club California, spilling music onto the street behind us.

"No. Home."

"Yeah? Can I come?"

"Ummm. I'm living in this house? With these bikers," I said, as if that explained everything.

"Let me in."

"Ruth." I tried to sound firm but affectionate. "I can't. I don't think they'd be cool with it. You know?"

She couldn't have been more shocked if I'd run her over.

The driver locked the door, sensing some portent of trouble.

"Let! Me! In!" She yanked the handle so hard the cab quivered.

I turned away and told the driver my address.

Ruth looked less angry than hurt. Had our past friendship meant nothing? But I'd come such a long way, I thought, moving forward while she'd stood still or moved back. In truth, she embarrassed me. Because she was a junkie and I smoked a pipe, which made me better than her, since my drugs didn't pierce the skin. Those who used needles were the real junkies. I had a house. I had pit bulls, a TV, a waterbed. I didn't do *heroin*, but if I let her into the cab I might as well start. Shame washed over me, and yet it didn't cleanse me of my imagined superiority. Simply put, I was being a bitch. Just then she sucker-punched me through the open window.

Certain actions require a response.

I got out of the cab. My first shot clipped her chin. I threw another right, hit her cheekbone, and we both fell to the sidewalk. She lunged with her nails. She scratched my face. She gouged me and bit my back.

As quickly as it began it was over. Ruth faltered down the street, half dancing away with the part of me that had giggled with her over handfuls of Valium chased with a shared can of Kokanee in the bathroom of Carey Road.

I got back in the cab. I sat in the passenger seat, breathing heavily. I took out my compact and surveyed my face in the pearls of street light. I looked up at the driver. "Do I look really bad?"

He shook his head. "No, no. You look, really, very okay."

I knew he was lying.

———

I hurried straight from the front door of my house to the wash-room, avoiding everyone. It was bad enough being fifteen. People already thought your age made you stupid. Now, at best, they'd be right. At worst, the boys would laugh at me. I wasn't tough enough. For what? For them, my life, my house, my pit bulls; for fights that began before you'd even had a chance to take off your coat, kick your shoes away; for everything. Weak and undeserving, I washed away the blood and stared at my face from various angles, wondering how to conceal the raw red scratches across my cheek from lip to ear. The bite marks on my back throbbed. Fuck it, I thought. I needed my bed. I put my shirt back on and went to my room.

I will never see Ruth again. Seven years later, I'll open a news-paper and read that she's been arrested, which makes the paper because she's HIV-positive and had bit a security guard's finger to the bone.

Downtown, on the corner of Government and Yates, ten at night, spring of 1987. A man known on the street as Jimmy Page, a forty-something dope dealer, supplied Will with drugs. Story was, the last person to owe Jimmy Page money had opened his door to see him on the front step holding a Snap-on toolbox. Jimmy had calmly taken out a hammer as the man tried to run. Jimmy fol-lowed and beat the man unconscious. Now Jimmy's friend Julie and I stood on the corner smoking. After a bad fix she'd given herself cotton fever—the chills and a temperature that came from drawing the drug solution through a cotton ball filter. Julie looked bad: green, as if ready to vomit. She was saying "Man, I feel shitty" when Jimmy hopped out of a cab on the other side of the street and jaywalked toward us.

I thought, She must have called him. He must be taking her home. I couldn't have been more wrong.

He whipped something from his pocket. Small enough that at first I missed its glint, like a mirror. It was a blade and he held it to my neck.

"Shit, Jimmy," Julie said.

I froze. Will owed Jimmy money. For drugs. But they had that all worked out. They had a deal.

"Where's Will?"

"I don't know." Why was this on me?

"Calm down," Julie said.

She hopped up and down between us, waving her arms like a deranged jumping jack. "She's not *with* Will," she said.

It was true: I fucked him and bought his coke but we were a couple only in the loosest sense of the word. His debts were not my responsibility. He slept with whomever he wanted, and left our bedroom smelling like sex and cheap strawberry body spray. I couldn't be expected to be loyal or dutiful in the face of that.

"I'm going to kill him or I'm going to kill you."

He spoke with a slow, sickly sweetness.

"Jesus, Jimmy, leave her alone!"

"Five bills," he said, "before you leave tonight."

"It's okay, I can do it," I said, marshalling a courage I didn't have. I don't remember what I'd told Will I would do for him, or if I'd said anything at all. I might have kept it secret, holding in the knowledge like a drug created solely to fuel my sense of superiority. It's equally possible I'd told him in a way that dramatized my skill in taming the wicked. The lethal. I was after his love, and whatever had or hadn't said, my act would prove something to him: I was someone to respect.

At dawn, I took a cab from the track to where Jimmy lived. I fingered the cash I'd earned, $540, thumbing the bills.

I'd never been to Jimmy's house and was unprepared for the maniacally conventional teacups littering the kitchen table, the newspapers on the chairs, the wads of gum on the counters, the dying plants on the windowsills, the domesticity of the spaghetti-sauce-instant-rice-Kraft-Dinner clutter on the shelves caricaturing normal life.

"Jimmy's not here," the girl who answered the door said. "Toke?"

She returned to the nest of blankets on the couch. Only then did I see her baby wriggling wormlike among the folds. She began nursing, offering me her joint. I took it and sat down next to her, keeping my jacket on. I'd heard about this girl. Jimmy's "wife," at seventeen.

"You know I'm HIV, right?" she said.

I couldn't look at her. I stared at the TV, where Jean-Claude Van Damme obliterated villains, the requisite building of tension to hold the shitty plot together. "Yeah," I said. I felt sad for the infant: the shadows in the room, the mess, those tiny fists that closed on nothing but air.

The girl seemed pleased to be smoking with me and rocked back and forth with the infant in her arms. "You know how many people won't share a joint with me now?"

As soon as Jimmy walked in, I stood. "I have the five," I said, in case he thought I'd come to beg for more time. Shaking, I fumbled with the money.

He laughed. Poured me a coffee.

"I'm, uh, good."

He put down the cup, crossed the room, and picked up the baby. He walked toward me smiling. "You want to hold him?"

He offered me the squirming bundle. Was this the same man who'd tried to knife me? The same man who'd nearly beaten someone to death with a hammer?

"Nah, I got a cab waiting," I lied. I mumbled a quick goodbye and let myself out, onto a street of parked cars whose windshields were paisley with frost.

The next morning, crawling out of my covers, I remembered something. In all the excitement, I hadn't stashed away the two twenty-dollar bills that remained after paying off Will's debt.

My money roll wasn't wrapped up in the sweater where I hid it. I looked through another sweater. Another. I couldn't find it. I shook out crop tops, spandex, miniskirts; I flung my clothes across the room. I emptied every shelf.

Will came to see what the thumping was all about. When I asked him where my money was he looked at me like I was crazy and shrugged. Then he went back downstairs, sat on the brown corduroy couch, and cooked up what coke remained on the coffee table.

Jay, a pimp from Winnipeg and an acquaintance of Will's, wore a pink suit and gelled his hair. In a household full of bikers, one of whom had slipped my bill roll into his pocket, his Jheri curls, diamond pinky ring, and tasselled leather loafers were glamorous. He danced in the glow of the wood stove, busting out all the new moves in our living room. His pink suit rippled with colour, and when he sat down beside me, his leg touching me on the couch, I felt a Taser jolt.

I recognize now that what I liked about Jay was his attentiveness, his solicitousness toward my roommates, the intimacy he seemed capable of bringing to our conversations.

About a month shy of my sixteenth birthday, the landlord evicted us for too many loud parties and we moved from Austin Avenue to a room at the Friendship Inn motel.

The night I turned sixteen, the room packed with people, all strangers to me, Jay took my hand.

All night I'd been doing drugs, lines, pills, whatever people threw at me as they yelled "Happy birthday!" Now, the crowd bearing down, I nodded, trying to conceal my gratitude, my eagerness, with long stately strides through the drunken rabble. Then I saw Will urgently shaking his head and mouthing "No." He'd told me that Jay was a pimp with two women working for him. That I needed to stay away from him because pimps were no good. They took all a working girl's money, and some set quotas.

I squeezed Jay's hand and he squeezed back—and that was all the reassurance I needed.

I followed him out the door.

He brought me to his own private room above the party, where we could talk, music thrumming through the floor. Knowing I'd be impressed, he showed me his jewellery, bags full of it, saying, "And this is only what I travel with."

He paid attention, to me alone, when we made love.

I started spending more time with him. In the months to come I found myself following him to the mainland and back, living wherever he wanted to station me, in motel rooms in Vancouver and Victoria. His sister lived in Vancouver in a brick apartment building near the Broadway track a few blocks from the Kingsgate

Mall. While he smoked joints at his sister's I'd work with middle-aged women, mostly addicts, some who still looked good.

I gave him the money I earned on the track, but the luck that had hit me with what felt like blunt-force trauma ran out. Jay no longer seemed as interested. The money I put in his hand each night didn't make him want to hang out with me. I'd stopped being the focus of his attention.

I was arrested for breach of probation in Vancouver. At the time I was wearing a satin camisole, a black satin blazer, and a pair of purple spandex pants.

After your arrest a female screw tells you to strip, puts on gloves to examine behind your ears, checks between your toes, runs her fingers through your hair, makes you open your mouth and lift your tongue, and bend over. You have to take a shower with Kwellada to kill any lice or scabies or crabs and to rid your face of makeup. They give you pants that look more like pyjamas. They process away your personality until you're no different from the page on which your pretrial report is printed, your life reduced to a paragraph, to black and white.

After being flown back to Victoria in handcuffs, I found myself in Youth Court. In a room full of steno pads, business suits, and briefcases, I stood charges. The judge sentenced me to four months in youth jail.

Black Rope Hell and Upside-Down Prison

From within the walls of Victoria's Youth Custody Centre, a maximum-security jail for young offenders, you couldn't see grass or anything else green or alive, only the courtyard, a concrete square the size of a basketball court. Its walls were twenty feet high.

The jail's official capacity was about forty kids but it often held more than fifty. When that happened we couldn't shower more than once a week and some kids were sent to Oakalla, the adult prison on the mainland. What I knew of Oakalla I knew from stories. A boy from East Wing had a brother who'd been killed there.

East Wing had nine rooms. Most were six-by-eight shoeboxes made of concrete. West Wing had seven, and the one at the very end of the hall that I shared with two other girls was a little bigger than the others, meant to be a double. Our wing had a television we could watch on Saturday nights. We were allowed eight cigarettes a day, rationed on a strict schedule. And because the guards stored them in the freezer, each pack with our name written on it, the filter between my lips was always cold. As the weeks plodded into months, I tried to remember how liberated smoke tasted on the tongue, smooth and unrestricted.

Every time we swore a guard would say, "Drop and give me twenty!" Push-ups, military style, every time.

One of the boys told me about an older woman who'd tied him up by the wrists from the ceiling. Why he'd befriended me I had no idea. I refused to see all that he and I had in common. His helplessness, his confession that he'd slept with both women and men for money, churned my stomach.

At breakfast, as West Wing filed toward the cafeteria past the boys from East Wing who'd finished eating and now stood lined up against the corridor wall waiting for us to pass, people would take shots at this boy's face. His lips trembled as he was punched, but he never cried. His capacity to bear our violence was as macabre as the way his thin arms widened at his elbows. Why didn't he fight back? Why did he let himself be treated like shit? People saw that as begging for more. The bigger boys were only giving him what he wanted when he turned a red and swollen cheek.

If a guard caught a boy he went to the Blue Room: a cell, painted blue, that had nothing inside it and whose function was to calm those who were out of control. Left to run its course, a tantrum would become self-inflicted violence: spitting, kicking, punching walls. Until at last, with broken hands and torn, bleeding knuckles, the boy would lie exhausted on the floor.

A guard named Jane introduced me to Hermann Hesse and *Siddhartha*. Siddhartha moved through different walks of life to become wise, to reach enlightenment. He'd bucked the system. And he'd won. As did Robin Lee Graham, who wrote *Dove* after he'd circumnavigated the globe on a twenty-one-foot sailboat starting when he was sixteen, the same age I was now. I read both books cover to cover until the pages were stained with my fingerprints and the endpapers had fallen off. I wanted that. The world. Adventure. Without the sailboat that had been stolen from me when my first boyfriend had cheated, but a knowledge-seeking expedition nonetheless.

I had a job in the laundry.

Volunteered to push the library cart.

Every morning our wing was awakened not by an alarm but by "Welcome to the Jungle" by Guns N' Roses blaring over the loudspeakers.

We'd race to the clothing room to grab a new pair of pants and a T-shirt.

Then we went to "school."

I acid-burned glass, carved wood, made moccasins. I drew—and won a prison art contest.

I'd sketched a mother and child in a Madonna and Jesus pose using charcoal, smudging lines, cross-hatching with the sharpest pencil I could find.

I returned to Jay when I was released from juvie, catching a ferry to Vancouver with the clothes I'd worn when I was arrested. I didn't care how the tourists on the boat stared at my spandex pants or my satin blazer. *This* was the beginning of adventure. *Now*. I'd kiss the deck. Let people watch. All I had was my clothes, and my freedom.

Jay picked me up. He picked me up like a misplaced wallet and slipped me back into his life.

Within a few weeks he began ignoring me again, and I knew I'd made a mistake coming back.

I spent many nights alone wondering what I'd done wrong, finding answers in the generic environment that mid-range hotels can provide with their patterned carpet, their floral designs, their impersonal still lifes framed in fake wood above an empty dresser. Each room the same as the last.

Jay belonged to me. After all, Julie, my wife-in-law, lived in Winnipeg, over two thousand kilometres and a twenty-four-hour drive away. *Wife-in-law* referred to the other women in a man's harem, in his stable. But I pretended I wasn't sharing him. That I wasn't in a state of competition for his affection. I hated the Other, imagining how I measured up. Since she was in another city, the distance meant I could dissociate from her, sidestep questions like "Did she fuck him better tonight than me?" "Whose trap was bigger?" "Does he like the smell of her hotel room better than mine?" I'd spray perfume on my comforter, my pillowcases. I wanted every aspect of Jay's time with me to be comfortable, alluring, so much so that he'd be unable to pull himself away. And if he did, the lingering scent on his clothes, in his hair, would force him to carry my memory.

The worst thing a pimp could do was relinquish his time without charge. Chat over a drink with a secretary, a dental hygienist, a stripper; invite her to dance, ask her to the movies. On the house. Not because it meant cheating on his ho but because pimps, like prostitutes, required payment for their time. To paint the town with a woman who wasn't putting money in your hand proved several things. That such a man was a "popcorn pimp," as bad for your health as junk food. He lacked the skill to transmute a woman's "square" life into a gold mine. His personal pot at the rainbow's end. Accomplished pimps influenced women to the degree that they believed the choice to stand on a corner and rent their bodies to the highest bidder was their own. Anyone who craved love was a target. Anyone with a backbone, who threw themselves all chips in. How could love—its acquisition—not be a noble pursuit?

Jay's reputation for being a "free fucker" was a concern. On the track a girl told me she'd seen him with another woman. It wasn't that this girl cared about me; it was that Jay's rule-breaking damaged my position, standing, and prestige on the track, and that she took pleasure from cutting me down.

"I seen him dancing with some girl at the Biltmore," she said. She lifted her chin in challenge. She wanted to convince me, half through intimidation and half through the semblance of girl-on-girl bonding, to join her family, to choose her pimp and leave mine. She added, raising the stakes, "I seen him sucking face with her at the bar." As if to say, What are you going to do about it?

"Probably someone he was trying to bump," I said, lamely defending him. My heart wasn't in it. I imagined his tongue invading her mouth like an alien mandible. I felt small, an ant carrying a load heavy enough to push me into the ground.

My back aching and my feet blistered from my cheap shoes, I caught a cab home to the motel. During the short ride from Broadway and St. Albert to the City Centre on Main Street, I wondered what had captivated him about the girl at the Biltmore. What made her so much better than me? I'd formed a picture of her in my mind, piecing her together from those who strutted their stuff with more jiggle and sway than any ho I knew. Who drank at table after table like a bee dropping into different flowers to suck back as much nectar as possible, not caring which man paid. Who laughed too loudly, throwing back their head. Who lived never looking over their shoulder. Bold, crass, white-trash armour thrown over the heart on their sleeve, inches of black eyeliner, the feathered hair, the tight jeans, the tasselled leather jacket, the boots. Why her? Why wasn't he satisfied with me?

In the years to come I'll wear the scars of competition. I'll recognize the chip on my shoulder for what it is, but I'll be unable to rid myself of the belief that I'm second best. That I'm less valuable. That if a man goes elsewhere to find what he needs it's my fault; I must be deficient in all the ways that matter—beauty, youth, obedience, an intuitive ability to predict what he wants. That I'm not enough to encourage him to keep his dick in his pants. These temptresses must have tapped in to some secret.

Today I can say that I hadn't made Jay cheat on me with a square girl. That I hadn't created my own pain.

But back then, by making up an excuse for him, by nodding my head at the girl on the track, I *was* creating my own pain. The actions were his. But the choice to stay was mine.

I rode the few blocks to the motel with a tight ball in my stomach. I'd try to change: I'd run him baths, light his cigarettes, pick up food for him at four a.m. when he woke me from a sound sleep to say he was hungry . . . I could do better. Become more pliable. More obedient. More "down." When girls spoke of me on the track, other hos would say, full of awe and respect: "Jay's woman? Props, man. She's one down ho."

I turned my key but the door wasn't locked. I thought, Maybe he knows I found out; he's bought roses, is waiting to say sorry; I'll see his heart changed. I pushed open the door and saw Jay.

And another woman, who gasped and shuffled in the blankets as she tried to pull them over her breasts.

Jay smiled at me and lit a cigarette.

"What now?" he said while the girl, still clutching the blanket to her chest, searched for her clothes among the tangled sheets. "Bring us a glass of water?"

No shame on his face. His brazenness stunned me. Had he wanted me to see? To show me he could do anything?

I thought about hitting the pretty blonde but stomped out of the room instead. He followed me. We glared at each other in the parking lot and then began yelling, cars forced to drive around us, me in my ho clothes, him shirtless in bare feet and the pyjama bottoms he'd pulled on.

"You're nothing but a big fucking headache," he said, "you know that?"

Because I'd caught him?

"Fuck you."

Jay and the woman left in a cab. Determined not to lose sleep, I crawled into bed, the motel sign glowing red through the window. The parking lot traffic had died down. I tried to shut my eyes and push the affair out of my mind by reassuring myself that Jay understood the mistake he'd made. By telling myself he'd never dare do it again. My mind flashed to the boy at juvie and for the first time I realized what I'd hated about him: it had been like looking in the mirror. Digging deeper under the covers, losing myself to exhaustion, I felt something touch my toe. I leapt out of bed and shook out the blankets. Then I saw it. Silky and black. Her panties.

I had to get out. I couldn't breathe. I packed, or rather, threw my belongings into whatever luggage I had at the time. A mixture of tote and garbage bags. Maybe a suitcase. What I remember is the conviction that I had to flee. Like a wild animal. Under attack.

I opened the door and stepped out into the pre-dawn stillness. With the weight of my bags straining my shoulders, I sighed, looked left and right. Good girls could handle anything. Could withstand anything, like Siddhartha in Hesse's book—still as a forest effigy in the pouring rain, bearing up under the onslaught of the elements. I wanted to claim such strength as my own. Good girls rolled with the punches, turning them into a ballet, absorbing blows with a fluidity of movement I dreamed of.

I crossed the street and walked a few blocks to the motel of a girlfriend, Frances, who also worked the track. She commiserated, saying things like "Fuck, Suko." But it wasn't solace that I needed. Why couldn't she reprimand me? Say, "If only you'd lit his cigarettes, run his bath, made more money, this never would have happened." That could have marked my path as clearly as paving stones. Reinstated hope instead of taking it out back and shooting it.

I had to admit it: in Siddhartha's position I wouldn't have lasted a day.

I wouldn't survive. Not like this. What was I willing to do to toughen myself up?

The next morning, Slim, Frances's Seattle pimp, gave me a ride to Vancouver. Frances sat in the passenger seat, twiddling with the car stereo.

"You got to give him something to bring you along," she'd said the night before. "How much money have you got?"

"My whole trap. Jay left before taking it."

"Kay. I'll ask him. He'll probably charge you about fifty dollars."

Deal made, we now sat on the car deck of the *Queen of Nanaimo* ferry boat, seagulls plying the sky while we listened to Keith Sweat in Slim's tinted-down Cadillac and smoked.

Over the next few weeks, I renegaded. On Broadway, numbers of renegades worked alongside dumpsters, their take too low to interest most pimps. Only downtown, one block from Granville Street's neon and nightclubs and theatres, could a girl earn a good living. There, women stood on display with the poise of supermodels in leather and fur, swinging designer purses. Tricks paid double and triple what the junkies on Broadway charged.

Fast money, my alter ego rationalized, was more honourable than slow money, and working the streets more honourable than, say, flipping burgers for minimum wage. You gave up less time for a bigger return. If you had to sell out, wasn't it nobler to sell out for big money?

So, despite knowing that the entire block bounded by Seymour, Helmcken, Richards, and Nelson streets was controlled by pimps, that renegades would be a target there, I moved downtown.

When asked "Who's your people?" I'd answer Slim. Or I'd say my man was down in Vegas, or doing the cross-Canada circuit with a wife-in-law. Sometimes I'd say he was in the pen, doing a seven-year stretch. Of the three, that last lie met with the least resistance. Jaded working girls wanted to believe in this long-suffering-shaped love. They found hope in the idea that to suffer long would provoke the kind of gratitude that came shaped as a wedding band, sacrifice redeemed.

It was Frances who told me that Jay was coming back to town. "Girl . . . ," she said, and didn't finish the sentence. She didn't have to. I'd be in a heap of trouble if he found out I'd used his name. I panicked.

Repeating Spring

Frances suggested I meet another friend of hers, and that we all go out for dinner together.

Then she hesitated. "But you don't even know what he looks like."

"Is he fine?"

She curled her fingers into the okay sign and then fucked the hole with her other hand, chortling.

Her friend Avery had a lisp and walked with a wiggle. His skin was the colour of fudge-flavoured caramel squares. His moustache, beginning to show filaments of silver, made him look like my favourite R&B singer Morris Day.

We went to a restaurant on the harbour. The waiter hovered to refill your water glass, let you smell the wine. Avery sat to my right, his elbows on the table. He took up the room with his charisma. He was exuberant, and boisterous, and unashamed of being loud, black, and covered in gold chains. His eyes sank deep into me like anchors.

I admired his set jaw, darting eyes, laughter that suggested an "or else." I admired his tough-guy stance in a world I knew would stop at nothing to beat you down. More than anything, I think it was his eyes. They shared that trapped, manic look I'd seen in my own reflection. I circled the rim of my wineglass with my finger and tilted my body toward him, toward his sadness, like mine, that I could sense even when he smiled.

"The pimp in me is doing fine," he said, laying down his line of drag. "The man in me is looking for a woman to spend the rest of his life with."

I asked him if that meant I'd have to share him.

"Yes, I do have other women. Of course they're beautiful. But not like you, baby. Those other women are just ladders. If you want to travel the world, if you want to live in West Vancouver, then think of them as taking you where you want to go."

"Unless you're a woman who can make eight bills a day."

"Could that be you?"

"I don't deny it. I like to live well."

"But what I got to do to get that pocket lining. Do you think I enjoy having to make love to so many women? I'm waiting for rescue too, baby. If you were the one who could make eight bills a day, I could throw the others out like toilet paper. A million-dollar ho would complete me. We'd escape. Do everything. She'd never have to worry about sharing me. I keep a stable because I'm *forced*, when in essence I'm a one-woman man."

We went to a nightclub where he became the kind of person people would form a circle around, move back from on the dance floor so they could watch. The kind of man girls lined up to dance with. And when he was finished dancing, he was the kind of man other men slapped on the back with words of encouragement.

"You gonna hurt them girls."

"You tearing the place up!"

I chose to be with Avery, pretending it was a choice, pretending Slim wouldn't kick my ass. I had to choose someone.

It might as well be him. Avery set me up in the Robsonstrasse Hotel, asking whether I liked the place, strutting around in an expensive suit, spinning the keys of a rented sports car on his index finger. But I remember clearly the dread I'd known waiting for my father to enter the room with the ruler slipping away.

We drove to the West End, where Avery introduced me to his sister. I'd put on thick eyeliner and dark lipstick to mark that moment, the beginning of something good, something real. And to make myself look older. On the street, where so many wanted nothing to do with me because of my age, my youth felt like a curse, especially now that I had a pimp eleven years older than me. I'd lost too much to lose Avery over something as stupid as being sixteen. By law I was still a child, and most pimps would have nothing to do with girls younger than eighteen. For Avery, my age represented a criminal risk. I didn't see him as taking advantage of me. Instead I was grateful that I'd been given a break, a chance to prove my love and loyalty. I was eager to learn, ready to please.

His sister hugged me in the doorway of her apartment by the water. "She's so pretty," she said, glancing toward Avery approvingly. "She's so *pretty*."

The windows were shut up and the place stank of cat piss. Not even the pot smoke helped mask the acrid odour. As if seeing her place for the first time, in the way that fresh eyes, when a friend drops by, make you notice the mess you hadn't before, his sister said, "Your first set of furniture is supposed to be cheap and ugly, because you don't plan on keeping it." She explained that this was a pit stop on the road to success, the luggage she'd leave behind when she upgraded. Then she told me about the coffee table she planned to buy.

Over the following years I'd come to understand that the thrill came not only with the upgrade but with the jettisoning of the old. The ostentatious display of purging. Of emancipation.

Trick hotel rooms are always bathed in a cool, drab light. In the water-splashed mirror above the sink, I don't look that unhappy. Bright light makes tricks aware of every minute passing. The lights are also on for safety. No one tells me these things. I learn on my own.

As a sex worker, you've got to be tough, you've got to assume that every man is a serial killer. Forget his better nature or his nobler self. Don't fool yourself into thinking people have a capacity for self-control, for compassion, for understanding. It'll get you into trouble every time. Don't let down your guard even for a second: what's on the line is too precious to leave to fate or destiny. It's nothing other than your very life, so you'd better not fuck around.

Don't, for instance, ever get into someone's car. Don't give him the chance to drive you wherever he wants to go. Because even if you think you could jump from a moving vehicle, have you seen what happens to a body that hits the pavement at fifty miles an hour?

Instead, make him park, then you both take a cab to the hotel. If he won't take a cab, don't do the date. Two or three or five hundred dollars isn't worth risking your life.

Go only to those hotels where you have protection. Parsa, the desk guy at the Golden Crown, keeps a baseball bat behind the counter.

Once in the room, never lock the door, never turn out the lights, never turn your back on a trick, which includes doing it doggy style, not that I would, because only nasty hos have sex rather than fake a lay, which cannot be done doggy style.

To fake a lay:

use two condoms

KY slathered between

lodge your hand in your ass cheeks, right against your perineum

guide his cock into the hole you've made.

Don't close your eyes,

accept food or drink,

leave a plate at a restaurant, even if you must go to the bathroom.

He could arsenic you,

put sedatives in your vermicelli.

I could go on, but I think you understand that the quicker you realize everyone's a predator waiting to stab, poison, bludgeon you, the sooner you'll stay safe.

I wasn't unhappy being a prostitute. Like breathing, or eating, or getting out of bed each day, working the streets was simply what I did.

People told me to smile more. "You look sad all the time," they'd say.

"That's just my face," I'd respond. I meant it. Even on some nights when I swore that if someone offered me thirty bucks or "a real good time" again I'd pop them one. Or when people stopped by my corner and wanted to chat. Jesus Christ on a stick. I wanted to tell them, "If you walked into a bank you wouldn't stop and chat with the teller for ten minutes. And if she didn't give you more than the time of day you wouldn't call her a cold bitch and ask *Why are you girls so heartless?*" I couldn't explain that "I'm on my J-O-B." They didn't get it. *Why can't you be human and chat?* God. Pissed off? Yes. But sad? I told myself I didn't feel sad at all.

I was about to head home for the night when a muddy white Honda Civic pulled into the parking lot. I walked down the alley on Helmcken Street, and when the guy unrolled his window I stuck my head in. Empties littered the backseat, which was covered by a purple and green Mexican blanket.

"You looking for some company?" I said.

"Maybe."

"Why maybe? You know you want to."

"It depends."

"On?"

"How much."

"The minimum for a nice time is one-twenty."

"What does that get me?"

"My hotel's only five minutes away."

"A blow job?"

"We don't discuss anything like that here."

"But I can get a blow job, right?"

I stepped back, lighting a smoke. "See, prostitution is not illegal. But soliciting for the purpose in a public place is."

"Can you tell me in the car?"

"Just park and we'll get a cab to my hotel. It's only five dollars away."

"But I have a car."

"There's no parking down by the hotel, silly."

We flagged a cab and had gone less than a block when I saw the lights of a police car behind us. The cab pulled over. In the months to come I'd find out the trick was a cop, but that night the police pretended to arrest us both. They handcuffed him on one side of the car and brought me over to the other side.

A female officer arrived and seemed excited about getting to know me.

"Do you have a boyfriend?" she asked.

"Of course."

"Really?" Smiled. "What's he like?"

"He's dreamy."

"What's his name?"

"Why don't you ask him? He's hiding. In my purse."

She narrowed her eyes. "Hands on the car. Spread your legs."

She dumped the contents of my handbag onto her hood as if to find him in there. They booked me into Willingdon, the youth detention centre in Burnaby.

The beds were laid out in two rows; that we were sleeping dormitory-style had something to do with renovations, the guard had said.

"Didja know C.J.?" A heavy-set girl with black hair had pressed her face so close that her breath touched my cheek. To distract her I turned to the stainless-steel counter above the sinks and started lining up my beauty products, ones the police had allowed me to put in a small bag to bring with me while they were searching my room.

"C.J.," she hissed again. "She's from Vic."

"From juvie," I said. "Yeah, I know her."

"She told me you beat her up."

"As if." C.J. was huge. She was also my friend.

"Are you calling me a liar?"

She watched me wash my face. My hands shook, but the splashing motions disguised it. I was an expert in hiding things. Still, my fist down in the basin, my eyes closed—this was foolhardy. I opened my eyes quickly and dried my face off.

Then I lay down on my assigned bed. My back was to the girl but I could sense her standing there, looking down at me.

"You're a fucking hooker," she said. "That's *stupid*."

I looked up to see her resting her hands on her big fat gut. That's when I realized. She wasn't fat; she was pregnant. Very, very pregnant.

"What makes you so special?" I asked. "How are you going to take care of your baby?"

Her jaw dropped, her hands fell. I was going to add *Go plan a B&E. Leave me alone*, but the look in her eyes made me regret what I'd said. I rolled onto my side, away from her.

Then I felt something land in my hair. Wet, heavy, warm.

One by one, each of the girls in the dormitory took a turn spitting on me.

The rest of the night unfolded quietly. Before falling asleep I thought about the girls on the track, how different they were from that fat pregnant girl, how girls like her didn't see us the way we working girls saw ourselves. It had never occurred to me before that no one else would ever appreciate our greatness.

They released me three days later, on an undertaking that included a red zone—a four-block no-go surrounding Seymour, Nelson, Helmcken, and Richards streets. My trial was set for July, three months away, during which time I wouldn't be able to work the high track. Many pimps would have fired their woman, or abandoned her for the duration of her red zone. But Avery let me stay home, supporting me with the money his other women earned. It never crossed my mind that this was a business investment. I thought, This is something. Something real, like love.

He used to say we'd be together forever "unless I kill you or you kill me, and baby, believe me, I would do time for killing you." I thought this was romantic. Some months earlier, while living at the Robsonstrasse, I'd been working day shifts. One afternoon at home I was wearing a sweater from Holt Renfrew, given to me by a trick. I didn't like its beige colour, but I was fond of cashmere and I liked that it had the label of an expensive store sewn into the collar. I don't remember what started the fight, but suddenly I was hanging by my neck from the living room wall, Avery's hands around my throat, and what I remember most isn't feeing hurt, or hate, or even a change in the idea that Avery loved me, but simple amazement. A bone-deep surprise to discover that people did this to each other. My cigarette burned uselessly in my hand as I hung by my neck in Avery's grasp, the smoke spiralling. I could have butted it out in his eye. At the time, it didn't occur to me. Instead of burning Avery, the cigarette's cherry singed my sleeve. It wouldn't be until the next day that I'd notice the hole in the sweater, the one that had somehow made me feel respectable. I sat down in an armchair to stitch the edges back together with the wrong-coloured thread.

It was easy to split myself in two. Shadow and self. I'd been doing it my whole life. Being hurt at the hands of a loved one was not an option for my alter ego. When assaulted she had a knack for rationalizing away her own victimhood. While I may have curled into a ball and cried, my alter ego did not, simply by refusing to look at her injuries. The denial of her own suffering helped her support the illusion that she was in control.

Love, she thought. *Love the sinner, hate the sin.* The Hamar people, she told me, say that women with scars are as strong as lions. They practise ritual beatings, and the bonding that occurs between aggressor and victim, the scars left behind, serve as proof that someone cared enough to hurt you.

Sometimes the beatings came every month. In the early days, my foreknowledge helped me accept them—knowing they were about to happen, their predictability like the rising sun, somehow freed me from my fear of them, of the results.

Avery hated the thing inside him as much as I did. What "made" him "explode" he said, controlled him, not the other way around. Telling myself that Avery had a mental illness, true or not, meant that instead of anger or self-pity I felt compassion for him.

"I know I'm bad. But I want to change. I want to be good. Good the way you're good."

I'd do anything I could to help him. He needed me. Anything it took.

I could see his pain. "I'm afraid," he confessed. "I don't want to be a failure. In your eyes."

He cried in my arms, and I couldn't have felt more tenderness toward anyone.

"You are good," I repeated, stroking his hair. He needed my love, my understanding, my faith in him. "You are good."

And despite his violent tendencies, Avery did make me feel loved. He made me feel special by telling me stories of his abusive childhood and broken home, secrets he'd never told anyone else.

He was not a closed man or a private man or even a reserved man. Still, no one knew his secrets. Or no one but me. Whatever else my pimp was, his rules of engagement were clear. He awarded me attention and affection. For the first time in my life I was the axis around whom someone's life revolved. My old habits—the counting, the ritual touching—fell away in his presence. In return, all I had to do was pay him.

He moved with the grace of a dancer, his perfectly proportioned limbs, not overly muscular, carrying within them a kinetic intelligence, whether he went to the gym or not. He wore G-string underwear in a variety of colours: silver with gold stars, electric blue Lycra, teal with snaps at the sides.

Sometimes I braided his hair into tiny squares that spiked from his head like electrical wires.

I'd pull on each one. "Loves me, loves me not."

We could go to Safeway together, rent movies, ride his motorbike, and not argue for hours. We didn't need to act at being domestic: we were in love. He bought me diamond tennis bracelets while his other women went to work in leggings and plastic shoes; I wore the equivalent of what people spent on rent in a year. Avery took me dancing. I ate lobster whenever I liked.

He infused me, woke me up with his drawing in and pushing away, his telling me he loved me and then what I needed to do to win it, as if it were a race: Stick it out longer than any of the other five girls. Make him more money. Be more down. Help him with his—our—goal by procuring even more girls. That way we'd reach the finish line faster; the $500,000 we'd need to retire.

When I thought of Jay, or even Luna from school, I couldn't remember who I'd been with them. That life seemed like the leftovers of a meal, scraped clean off the plate, tossed out without a thought.

I usually took a cab to work, but sometimes Avery drove me on his motorcycle, the wind against my bare legs, the summer air on my shoulders, the accelerating pace of the pavement beneath my knees when we rounded a corner. I loved the heart-thumping speed of the bike, the tremble of metal between my thighs, my quickening breath because of it.

Yet when we had sex, I couldn't kiss him. We'd quickly developed beyond a normal pimp–ho relationship, but our sex was mechanical. In my dreams I saw him unbuttoning my blouse and letting his fingers linger. I saw myself riding him, sucking his cock, telling him what to do and how I liked it. In real life I lay beneath him like a plank, silent, fighting the thought that to enjoy was to take part in evil—to expose a vulnerability that, even while naked, must stay hidden. To enjoy was to break open, break apart, make it easier to be taken away in pieces.

There we were, our hopes set aside. Avery had wanted to be a dancer in music videos. Not only could he dance, he could sing. He serenaded me in the privacy of his car driving down Cambie Street's tree-lined boulevard, Blood, Sweat and Tears playing on the stereo.

Our dream was to move to a small town. Buy land and a trailer. Start a business there, something down to earth. was where most Local prostitutes wanted to end up in West Vancouver or the British Properties or Shaughnessy. But not me. I didn't want to *end up* anywhere—least of all surrounded by society's symbols of success. It was never wise to think too much about the future, but I did. All I wanted was space. A little land, room to write. A kid or two. And if our lives felt a little like driving to our destination in the dark with no headlights, then it also felt like the stars were following us, brighter because of the dark.

Bridge of Helplessness and
Chamber of Flames

Frances and I wound through the drunk, designer-clad couples that spilled from Richard's on Richards nightclub. Frances had come to my place once to braid Avery's hair into cornrows. She didn't bore me like other hos who talked about what car they planned to buy next. We talked about cooking and the artistry of her hairstyles, not which salons sold the best product. We were approaching the corner when we saw the jumper. The woman clutched her balcony railing in the crook of her arm, wavered four storeys above the sidewalk, balanced on one leg. The wind lifted her hair off her back, making her look, for a moment, like an angel in flight. She swung her other leg over the street, then did a little dip as if testing the water of a swimming pool with her toe.

As if this was the most ordinary thing in the world, Frances passed me her smoke, turned her hands into a blow horn, and called, "Come on down. I'll buy you a drink!"

"Yeah, me too!" I added.

Yuppies pressed each other off the sidewalk and onto the street for a better view. The crowd blew into their hands, hopped from one foot to the other, bored like people at a lousy movie. Where were the cops? On a Friday night the usual order of things was a cruiser every second car—they'd picked a crappy time to grab Chinese food.

"I'll bet she's *drunk*," came a voice from the crowd.

"Squaw," said another.

"Come on!" Frances called in her loudest voice. "Come down from there, now!"

The woman's pointed foot swept over the crowd like a ballerina at the barre.

A nice-looking dude in a suit lit a smoke. Then he said, "Jump already." A clubber from Richard's. Why'd he say it? Was he sore because he had no girl to go home to? Or because he'd had one and lost her? Anger wanting a victim? Maybe before now he didn't even know he had it in him.

Then more voices joined in. They grew in volume. I shook my head, unable to believe the scene that was unfolding.

"Jump, jump, jump!"

Four storeys above, she swayed.

"Jump, jump, jump!"

Who *were* these people? I looked around and didn't see devils. Just ordinary individuals who, in between chanting for this woman to jump, talked about other things; I heard snippets about Did's Pizza and would the Canucks make it to the playoffs?

Lori, a working girl we shared the corner with, appeared beside us. "Is she going to do it or what?" she said, drumming her fingers on her crossed arms. The commotion was making us all lose business.

Frances yelled, "Come down! This instant!"

The woman did. By letting go. She released her grasp on the railing and fell through the air as silently as a stone, and when she hit the sidewalk her legs, arms, and shoulders seemed to fold neatly on top of themselves, like a bedsheet.

For a second no one spoke. Her fall, her crumpled body, had cast a spell. Everyone's breath hung like a white stain against dark night air. Then the silence was broken by someone asking, "So is she dead?" She lay unmoving. Whatever spell her fall had cast disappeared and people rushed in to form a circle around the body. Someone took off his coat and threw it over her.

A man nudged her face with the toe of his shoe. "Too bad," he said. "She was nice for a squaw."

"I've got to sit down," I said.

Frances and Lori followed me into the Korner Kitchen.

As usual, the coffee shop was full of girls with black sable coats and designer purses and compacts brought out over tables whose tops were graffitied and cigarette-burnt and whose undersides were dotted with chewing gum. They fixed lipstick and powdered their noses next to bar types who wore their Movado watches on the outside of their shirt cuffs. Someone was yelling for off-sales.

I sank into the softness of a booth. I wanted it to swallow me, absorb me, take me away. I needed the safety of four walls, the familiarity of the tufted seats, the glass pane separating me from what had happened outside. But the rigid red vinyl against my back prevented me from imagining I was anywhere but here—in a cheap diner on the track where on any given night a girl was crying into the pay phone; another, in the bathroom pissing blood from a beating the night before; a third, sitting in one of the horseshoe-shaped booths at the front adjusting her waist-length hair to hide a black eye. Groups of women with brand-new breasts discussed the pros and cons of enlargement surgery, said things like "Yeah, now I got no feeling in my nipples. But, you know, whatever." Or rolled in the aisles like professional wrestlers, one woman vise-gripping another in her long, lean, tanning-salon-perfect thighs before grabbing a sugar canister and bringing it down on the other's head to the cheers and hollers of men who enjoyed telling others they hung out at a place where shit hit the fan and cat fights had more hair, bare flesh, and exposed breasts than a porno.

Sirens wailed in the distance, finally. My body trembled. Frances pulled the curtain shut for me.

Lori started going on about this trick.

A second ago we'd watched a woman fall to the sidewalk. How could Lori have forgotten so quickly? Hadn't watching a human being throw herself off a balcony affected her?

I closed my eyes but couldn't banish the image of the woman dropping through the silent black night.

"He didn't only *pay me*," Lori was saying, "but he wanted me to steal all his stuff, too. He told me to take his microwave and his stereo and his paintings off the walls. He even gave me the combination to his safe. And then, get this." She leaned over the table, lowered her voice. "After he gives me the combination, he says *thank you*."

"I don't think I could do that," Frances said.

Lori beamed, as if her superiority had been confirmed.

A part of me understood wanting to be cold, not wanting to be broken. I could acknowledge Lori's anger. We all had it. Anger against tricks, society, the world, sometimes even our pimps. The only thing that made us different from each other was what we chose to do with it. Where we put it when it got too big to swallow down.

Lori tossed a snapshot onto the table and said, "He *wanted* to be burned, starting with cigarettes." The burns around the man's nipples and on his inner thigh resembled the smallpox I'd seen in books. Even as part of me admired her thick skin, her fortitude, I grew nauseous.

"Did you leave him there?" Frances asked.

"*Duh*."

"You should have at least called 911," I admonished.

"Mother Teresa, here," Lori said.

Frances would have called 911. Frances would have waited with him until the ambulance arrived.

Frances hugged me and I broke. For the girl on the balcony, for the man in the photos who'd paid Lori to chain him to the bed and nearly kill him, for the world's hurts when beauty slipped away like a silken sheet.

"Of course I called 911, stupid. What do you think? I killed him?"

"We should have tried to save her," I said. "We should have saved her life."

Frances rubbed my shoulder. "That's right," she said. "Let it out."

My turquoise corset-backed dress from the Leather Ranch on Granville Street had cost $350. It came apart at the waist, and sometimes I wore the strapless top with black pants, other times the skirt with a satin blouse. The leather flared over the skirt waist and could be worn tucked up or down.

I owned a lot of leather, but I'd bought this dress before Avery, before handing over my money each night. Two years before, I hadn't yet realized that the ability to buy whatever you wanted immunized no one from despair. The leather's rich smell had wafted from the bag as the clerk passed it over the counter. Any misgivings I'd had about My Life So Far softened to the buttery texture of the dress it held.

No one had yet told me that a tight skirt with no stretch could hobble you, as the original hobble skirts had prevented house-wives from fleeing their kitchens and setting their cookbooks on fire in the streets. I'd yet to learn that a dress that can't be hiked up when it's time to run can kill you.

I was seventeen now, and, having worked for two years, profi-cient at spotting trouble. I should have known better, but nothing twigged my radar when the date asked if we could go to the Biltmore instead of the trick hotel.

I went to his room, took his money. Still wearing my turquoise dress, I excused myself and retreated to the bathroom, where I hid his money under the insole of my shoe.

I'd been giving him a fake lay for a couple of minutes when he grunted and stopped. I thought he was taking a break. But when he sat up silently next to me, trying to hide the condom hanging from his flaccid penis, it was clear that he'd come. I have no mem-ory of whether I tried to cheer him up, since it wasn't the first time this had happened with a date.

Sometimes if you stay calm, a date on the edge of freaking out will mellow. So I lit up a cigarette. The bonus was having to cross the room to lay my hands on my purse, which positioned me closer to the door. Still, my exit was blocked: he stood between me and my possibility of escape. The heavy burgundy curtains were tightly drawn. The room was suffocating.

"Hey. You're not done," he said. "You're not going anywhere until I get another lay."

I explained to him that he'd paid the minimum. I'd be happy to stay if he wanted more time. All he had to do was go to the bank machine. I'd even go with him. I told him all this as I was dressing.

"Fuck that. You're gonna give me a lay for free."

"It doesn't work that way."

I felt the roughness of the carpet against my cheek before I realized he'd smacked me down. I tried to stand but he grabbed my ankles. I screamed, struggling to throw him off my legs, but the leather skirt acted like a lasso; its binding tension meant that I couldn't kick hard enough to hurt him.

Then somehow I was up, and before he had another chance to grab me I brought the heel of my shoe down on his head as hard as I could. I dragged the embedded heel along his scalp, ripping open the flesh.

But he didn't go down like they do in the movies. He touched his head, blood beading from the wound, then looked down at his fingers. Deliberately, leisurely, he said, "You crazy bitch."

I opened the door and struggled as he tried to pull me back in; I battered his torso with my purse until he let go. Before I could jump out into the hallway he grabbed onto me. I held the door open with one hand and screamed.

"Shut the door, you little asshole."

You little asshole? Who says that?

"Shut the door. Or I'll kill you."

He had me by my hair. They're extensions, I thought. Glued on. They'd give. I'd tumble from his grasp and run, leaving him holding only my ponytail, wondering what had happened.

Security would come. Any minute now.

Bleed on the carpet. Leave DNA. Whatever you do, don't let the door shut.

No one heard my screams. Or they'd heard and didn't care to get involved.

Bite, kick, go down swinging.

An hour later, he let me go. Beat up and raped, he let me go.

I shook myself off, casting his memory away like dust from my shoulders. As I walked to a gas station I held up my head—*don't stumble, don't cry.*

A greasy metalhead wannabe sat behind the glassed-in counter on a bar stool.

"Can I see your phone?" The words rolled like rubber in my mouth.

"The phone? Customers only. You buying something?"

"Yeah. A cab." I ran my fingers through my hair and chunks fell out.

"Whatcha doing later? I know a party."

Had everyone lost their mind?

"Don't you like to party?"

My dress, blood-spattered. My eye already swelling. I looked into my compact—my earrings? Fuck. Gone.

"Just kidding. Cat fight?" He winked. "Bet you kicked her ass." He paused. "Seriously, though. There's a pay phone on the corner."

I stormed out to the pay phone, dug in my purse to find a quarter. Goddammit. My change purse, like my earrings, was gone. I limped back to the gas station.

I bought a pack of gum, flipped the attendant the bird, made my way back to the phone booth.

When the cab came, the driver asked me to show my cash. I wasn't surprised. With my hair crazy and my clothes bloodied, I looked like someone who'd rip him off.

On the way home I noticed that the trick's blood on my dress wasn't red, like you'd expect, but forest green against the turquoise. I never wore it again.

———

I didn't look at Avery as I walked across the room toward the couch. The bump on my head hurt and my right cheek felt taut under my eye.

"You're home early," he said. He put down the video game controller and looked up. "What happened to you?"

"I had to come home. I wasn't going to go back to the track so the date could come looking for me. I got raped. But I made a couple bills," I added quickly, "before it happened."

I threw the money down on the coffee table. The bills sat there, an image of themselves on the mirrored surface. Avery lit a smoke as if deciding on a plan.

We'd rocket over on his bike and kick his ass.

Avery would make him pay. We'd rob him.

He was still sitting back in the couch. "Well?"

"I'm not going back," I said. He couldn't tell me to return to the track. I wouldn't.

"Your wife-in-law had a bad date, too."

I went into the bathroom and washed the cut beneath my eye. Not big, but I'd have a shiner tomorrow.

"I'll give you a call in the morning," he said.

I came out of the bathroom. "What?"

"I have to go spend the night with Gina. She's messed up."

My stomach dropped. Every part of my body was telling me to run, but I had nowhere to escape to. My face grew hot as I took a deep breath, measuring my words. "Because she had a *bad date*?"

"Yeah."

"What about *me*?"

"Well, here's the other thing. Gina's best friend in high school, she tried to kill herself tonight. Gina got the call a little while ago."

I could picture Gina alone in her apartment as she would no doubt like Avery to find her—sitting cross-legged on the floor, wearing one of his T-shirts, uncombed hair, eyes bulgy from crying. Playing him, I was sure, for his sympathy.

"Oh, for fuck's sake." I was stepping on thin ice but was too mad to care. "She's working you. Is that what I have to tell you to get you to spend the night?"

He draped a suit from the closet over his arm, then retrieved his eel-skin toiletry bag from the bathroom—the black one in which he kept his shaving gel and razor, Jheri curl spray and shower cap—slipping his hand through the lanyard so that it dangled from his wrist.

"If you walk out that door right now," I said, "then don't plan on coming back."

For a moment he seemed to think about it, resting his hand on the doorknob and taking a deep, sustained breath. Then he shrugged. "Okay. Later, then."

Later, then? How dare he call my bluff? Had the months we'd spent together meant nothing to him? I saw him walking out with all I'd invested up to that point. My expectations for tomorrow, our dreams for the business we'd talked about opening.

Without him I was nothing.

Without me he was nothing.

He couldn't do this to me.

He couldn't do this to himself.

I hurled myself at him in a panic. "No, don't." I pulled the door closed, heaving. "I'm sorry."

I fell to my knees. He joined me on the floor, then gathered me up into his arms. He rocked me while I sobbed.

After he'd gone, leaving me to all the ghosts of the brown hotel room, worse for the fact that clinging to the air was the scent of his cologne, I spilled my angst onto the page. I asked for answers about the nature of good and evil, the distance between souls, between the lines of what I already knew, asking for wisdom. I hoped, by rereading it all, to divine the answers between the spaces.

In truth, the pen was too soft for this world. The pen moved like prayer between supplicant and god, when it moved. But mostly the pen was quiet. The pen was quiet but the questions, they screamed in passing, like people on a rollercoaster. Piercing but unremarkable, part of the background, ambience.

One night, Avery was waiting to take me to work on his bike, a new rice-rocket CBR 600 we'd recently bought. It went so fast that when he'd accelerated on an open stretch, I'd nearly fallen off the back at 220 kilometres an hour. When I'd told him how my butt had come off the seat, still stunned by the g-force that had made my lips flap, he laughed.

A portent of danger to do with my outfit hammered at me. Avery drummed his fingers on the doorknob, waiting for me, but I couldn't ignore the warning's migraine-like insistence; I took off my dress and high heels and changed into tights, flat boots, and a short leather jacket.

He dropped me off on the corner. I was fluffing my hair, flattened by the motorcycle helmet, and watching his taillights recede into Vancouver's pink dusk when a truck pulled over. Noticing a police car down the block, I foolishly hopped in.

Right after I shut the door the man reached across the bench seat and grabbed me. He threw me against the passenger-side window and said, "You're going to fuck me."

As if money were the issue, I blurted, "Okay. But it'll cost you two hundred."

By now he'd pulled over. "For free."

I struggled to escape his grasp but he had a firm grip of my hair and kept slamming my head into the glass. In the midst of wrestling I unlocked the door, swung it open. He sped off again and I saw my chance to press down on the horn.

I punched and kicked and when he slowed for a busy intersection I made myself into a ball and rolled out onto the street.

I'd ended up on the outskirts of Chinatown. As I made my way back to the track, brushing off the road debris, it dawned on me that my leather jacket and tights had protected me from the pavement: I'd been able to jump from his truck because I was wearing clothes to fight, kick, and run in.

A man in a suit looked at me with pity and asked if I was okay.

"Do you want some company?" I asked.

This man had stopped to help me, but my anger had clotted and broken like thunderclouds. He read it. "I-I-I just think now's not the time."

"Don't you like me?"

"How about coffee?"

"What the fuck are you doing talking to me?"

I stormed off, clothing myself in a vestige of fury to hide how vulnerable I felt. I'd allowed the assault to happen. To reclaim any remnant of self-respect, all I could do was rage.

I didn't need God. I could read signs.

After that, I looked to mysticism for answers.

Feng Shui.

Divination.

The Tarot.

My Chinese horoscope.

Poems, condensed, full of imagery.

When I turned up at home my pimp put a glass of wine in my hand and ran me a bubble bath. He told me I was amazing, brilliant, and that "You've never looked so fine," as many times as I needed to hear it.

Underworld Mansion

We moved hotels every few weeks. I had two grey vinyl suit-cases, a smaller burgundy Samsonite, a garbage bag filled with clothes, another bag for my hot rollers, blow-dryer, purses, and stilettos. The stilettos' steel tips were so worn down they were more like knife blades than heels—not only did they puncture the plastic when I'd heave the garbage bag to the car but they also left holes in the trunk lining. More than once they'd cut my arms. Looking at the gashes those heels made provoked in me a mixture of disgust and embarrassment.

I envied the hos who did the circuit—Calgary, Toronto, Montreal, Vegas, Honolulu, Tokyo, sometimes with their men, sometimes alone—imagining them in airports with suitcases worth more than their plane tickets, wearing matching yet sensible three-inch heels. Avery had promised travel, and I was still waiting for it to happen. He'd taken my wife-in-law Gina to Winnipeg. He hadn't taken me anywhere.

Avery's luggage was no better than mine, but he did have a suit bag and the toiletry clutch made of eel skin. I hated that clutch and had even stood over it with scissors: it symbolized my wives-in-law and the pain they caused me. He also had a briefcase full of soul cassettes—Oran "Juice" Jones, Midnight Star, Parliament. He kept it locked. But I'd figured out where he kept the key, and after I listened to them I'd try my best to put them back in the same order.

We had no fixed address. Turtled all we owned from place to place. I wasn't sure how this made me feel.

When I was home I thought about the track, and when I was on the track I thought about home. With the money I earned Avery bought cocaine while I splurged on leather boleros and house-plants, frying pans we'd leave behind, stickers never removed.

We ordered room service or delivery—pizza or Chinese—or we ate leftover popcorn from a movie we'd gone to the evening before, or burgers for days on end. Or we'd drink two litres of root beer and call it dinner, or a half-dozen candy bars, or a box of licorice. Overflowing ashtrays and room-service trays covered our floor. We'd have tomato soup and fries or French toast with peaches and roasted almonds topped with whipped cream and maple syrup. Then I'd dress and go to work on the track.

Between the spring of 1988 and the spring of 1989 we moved hotels an average of once a month, sometimes back and forth between Vancouver and Victoria. Hotels always found a reason to kick us out. The Robsonstrasse, the Huntingdon Manor, the Helm's Inn, the Century Plaza, the Pacific Palisades, the Comfort

Inn, the English Bay Hotel. We never lived any place long enough for it to feel like home. The year I was seventeen we lived in at least ten different places, including the Century Plaza Hotel, where we stayed longer than anywhere else.

It advertised itself as "the only all-suite hotel in the city." We lived on the twenty-sixth floor. The suite was large enough for a living room with a couch, a loveseat, and a coffee table; off to the side were a kitchen and a small dining area. A queen-sized bed, comforter, pillows. The hallway glowed a soft rose colour and the carpet quieted the click of my heels.

Avery wore a plastic shower cap to protect the couch and pillow-slips and all the other things he greased with his Jheri curl spray.

Our corner suite overlooked much of downtown. The balcony side looked over the bay toward the mountains—our future like our view, limitless. We paid for the room nightly at the front desk in a chandeliered lobby. But I couldn't pretend it wasn't a hotel, I couldn't pretend I was *home*.

Avery told the desk clerks we'd just arrived from L.A., owned an entertainment agency, and were looking to buy a condo in Vancouver. Later, swimming in the hotel pool, I pretended these lies were true. Imagined how it would feel if it were true.

Because the truth was I had a boyfriend who wore Armani, who'd spent my trap on a new sports car. The truth was pimps didn't retire, square up with their ho, and live happily ever after, and it was unlikely that my dream of co-owning a legitimate business with him would go anywhere. But Avery never disagreed with this goal, even as he neglected to explain the logistics of how we'd reach it.

There was no accidental quality about how he didn't work me to the bone, dog me as other pimps did their women. Other hos sat in the Korner Kitchen bragging about who'd been beaten the hardest, who'd stayed out the longest. I refused to enter the contest for that evening's Ultimate Victim. I appreciated Avery even as he was using me. I loved his silly sticky notes, the way he looked hunched over a Sega game controller, engrossed.

A reactionary person is like a foot blister, and thin skin, unable to withdraw from the source of its pain, has two choices: bleed and fester or grow calloused, hard. The shoe, though the cause, isn't morally responsible. I couldn't watch shows or read articles that depicted prostitutes as being unfeeling or downtrodden by men.

It felt too true. As did its opposite. How could I be "hard" when I was obsessed with love and being lovable? An obsession rooted in childhood. And in the same way I'd worked to excel academically and athletically, I now earned money to garner attention.

Manipulating someone's weakness for personal gain is wrong. Still, in our world, to be pimped with kindness and decency amounted to the closest version of love we had. Avery wasn't the monster society thought he was, and neither was I.

I tried to read Evelyn Lau's work—she was a retired sex trade worker who'd gone on to become a successful writer—and I threw the paperback across the room.

Avery could change a windshield, detail a car. A decade earlier, before becoming a pimp, when I was barely out of kindergarten, he'd worked square jobs. His hands showed the creases and calluses of someone who'd fixed things under a hood. He could install a stereo system. This edge, *his* edge, would carry us out of the game.

I knew that, with my help, he could become the kind of person he deserved to be. Proud of himself.

I was too naive to understand that staking myself on his success could be used against me. If I'd bothered to think about it, I'd have seen what I had in common with the lobsters we threw in a pot, who never felt the boiling water until it was too late.

I could see him running his own shop, chatting with his employees in his garage with his arms crossed and his feet planted solidly on the ground. I'd do the paperwork. Avery said I was better at anything to do with paper. Money, forms. And he was right—he could barely spell, and would read magazines by looking at the pictures. I worked out five times a week, read library books on psychology, psycho-spirituality, gardening. Who needed a formal education when I was writing every day and making $150,000 a year?

Frances was three years older than I was. She turned twenty-one shortly after my eighteenth birthday. She was as tough as she was tender and as thoughtful as she was streetwise. She was my best friend. And like me, her gift of the gab had made her especially good at the upsell. We often worked together, performing doubles at the Golden Crown, a place that, no matter how dirty, always had clean linens.

Sometimes when tricks would ask what "someone like me" was doing on the streets, I'd say, "Because nowhere in the Western world is being a poet a paid profession," repeating something I'd read. Probably in a book Frances had given me.

She'd introduced me to J.D. Salinger, loaning me her mother's copy of *Nine Stories*. We'd shared our thoughts on his writing, and I'd given her my poems to critique. I wrote quatrains. Free verse. Villanelles in a binder with loose-leaf.

But one night Frances seemed out of sorts. She'd drunk enough

wine from the Korner Kitchen that she wavered in her step and
her cheeks had turned scarlet. Especially the scar under her right
eye, which would have been as ugly as a garden worm on anyone
but her.

We sat down with a trick on a bed at the Golden Crown. "Now
that we're in a private place we can explain your options. Like a
menu at a restaurant," Frances chirped in an unnaturally high
voice. "And then, the sooner we can take care of finances, the
sooner we can have fun."

Frances noted the trick's dubious expression and said, "Don't
worry about the place. We're the main attraction." Room 102
had Astroturf on the floor. It extended along the short hall that
led to the washroom, where we put the first $120 he'd given each
of us into our shoes for safekeeping.

She readied a washcloth at the sink and then let out a long,
unladylike burp. I was going to ask her what was wrong but
decided to wait until after the date.

Back in the room, I watched Frances cover the trick's penis
with soapsuds, touching it only through the washcloth. Then,
straining to keep her gaze focused, she unrolled a condom on his
half erection.

"Don't light a cigarette," she ordered him, sinking back on her
heels, semi-naked, her thighs open, breathing heavily through a
wrinkled nose. "Listen. It's your money. If you want to spend your
time *smoking*."

He looked at her, puzzled. "I started by giving you a hundred
and twenty each. And it's been just five minutes—"

"Oh, come on. Chop-chop." Frances weaved, trying to plant
her lips on his cock. "Lie back." She bobbed up and down, her lips
pursed like a fish.

Chop-chop? I raised my eyebrows. Frances wasn't tipsy, she was drunk.

"C'mon, Michelle, let's go," she said, using my street name. "He's not even *trying*." She faltered on the edge of the bed, her eyes hazily focused on the door.

She'd found out about a new wife-in-law the week before, and ever since she'd been drinking at work. I figured it was the stress. But I was on the verge of being fed up. We used to be a team. Now I had to weigh her liabilities against her assets.

I calmed the man down, telling him to feel sorry for Frances. "She lost a baby, miscarried last week," I whispered. I appeased him by saying little things about how unloved we as prostitutes felt in general, and how when a man seemed neither interested nor stimulated it felt even worse. My tactic in these situations was always the same: talk fast and keep talking. Pump their egos. Make it so that walking away would make them feel big. Bigger than killing you.

In the cab back to the track Frances told me she'd had seven abortions and that she couldn't have another.

"I know," I sighed. I'd heard it all before.

Frances sighed too, and patted her belly. "I'm pregnant again." She closed her eyes. For the moment she appeared content.

How many times had I thought about the vast possibilities of our future? I'd forget about Avery and Frances would forget about the man who'd beaten her so badly she'd locked herself in a bathroom and tried to slit her wrists to escape the pain. We'd pack our bags and hitchhike east, living off the kindness of truckers, sleeping our way where we needed to go. Or we'd buy one-way tickets to South America, fall in love with poetry-quoting leftists, and die fighting corrupt government. Or run away to the hills of California, where she'd grown up, and live freely, without clothes or disguise. Frances would give birth in a commune and I'd become old and wise, spouting adages like rivers. We knew each other inside out and could finish each other's sentences.

Much later, when Frances went missing I filled the pages of my journal with all the things I used to say to her over coffee in the Korner Kitchen as we waited for a cab back to the track from the trick hotels on Hastings. I told my journal what was on my mind, recorded the troubles I was having, and, rereading, tried to make sense of it all. The way Frances had. Tried to supply myself with recommendations and advice the way she'd always been able, in an uncanny way, to reflect my best thoughts. Coming from her, my half-baked ideas made sense. But what I seemed unable to do was offer myself the understanding and compassion Frances had always given me.

In the years to come there'll be occasional unconfirmed sightings. Avery swears he's seen her on the Surrey track. Fellow working girls say Hastings, or Broadway, or a drugstore aisle buying toothpaste. One night a woman calls for me on the Korner Kitchen pay phone. "No, she didn't leave her name or number," said the working girl who answered. "No message."

Gina, my wife-in-law, licked a dollop of mayonnaise off Avery's index finger. I sat on the couch at the Mansion after-hours across from her and downed champagne, thinking how I'd like to tighten my fingers around her neck.

The after-hours was an actual mansion in Shaughnessy, hidden by maple trees and a gated driveway in a neighbourhood of Spanish villas and imitation Tudor castles. How did I get here? Avery, taking us both out at the same time. A man got his respect when he kept his women in line, and nothing showed it more than taking them out as a pair, like cufflinks, he said. So why did it bother me? We knew what was what and what was real—he just had to spend more time with her because she wasn't as strong as I was, had so many insecurities.

"I love your new extensions, Gina." I smiled. "I'll bet hardly *anyone* can tell they're synthetic instead of real hair."

Gina's last pimp had cut off her hair in punishment. I should have felt sorry for her, but my sense of injustice at having to share my man in the first place made that impossible. She'd brought it on herself. How could she have tried to kiss him when her breath had smelled like condoms?

Avery slammed down his glass. I'd been doing this all night long, fucking with her, and this was the final straw. He grabbed my elbow and wrenched me outside.

The patio flagstones held onto the heat of the day and felt warm under my bare feet, but the air, cold and dry, rested on my shoulders like the hands of a distracted masseuse.

"What's your problem?" Avery hissed. "Can't you see what I'm trying to do here?" He flicked ash from his cigarette into a planter. "We've been through this."

"What about me?"

"Yeah? What *about* you?"

"You haven't even danced with me." I sobbed quietly. "Maybe I wanted to dance, too."

"I don't think you should have any more to drink tonight," he told me.

I lowered my head, sure everyone was watching through the

long, tall windows. Gina would see; everyone would know that I'd been put back in his pocket.

Through the glass I glanced at pimps reclining on sofas, hos snacking on plates of curried goat. Up the spiral staircase were bedrooms with massage oils, dildos, collars, and chains. A man was leading two women into one of the rooms, spilling red light into the hallway.

I wondered if Avery had ever taken Gina up there, their giggles fading as he closed the door behind them. Once, in anger, I'd even asked him, "How *do* you guys fuck? I mean, literally. She's six and a half feet tall."

For the past few months I'd been painting elaborate pictures of what she might be like in bed, trying to put myself in his position, imagining what he found unique about her. Then I imagined myself, how it might be, could be, the next time he spent the night with me. Could I outdo her?

Not while scared of caressing his cock, not while lying there flat as a surfboard.

All I ever did was lie there. I had no idea why I couldn't engage with the act, even when I wanted to. When I was alone in the hotel room, waiting for Avery, the idea of sex could be so lovely. But once he showed up with his suit bag and eel-skin toiletry clutch I'd begin thinking of the slickness with which Gina and he became one, the painless way their bodies fit together with the ease of puzzle pieces, and I'd be overcome by feelings of personal failure that invaded our already infrequent love-making.

That night, after Avery dropped Gina off at home, he turned to me in the backseat. "Why are you sabotaging my game? How many times do I have to explain? I'm working for *our* money."

"You're acting like I'm a tip," I said, "and not your main at all." I was still drunk enough to put up a fight, to dare try.

At a red light I hopped out of the car. I heard his tires screech behind me but I didn't look back.

He must have parked and gotten out, approached me from behind. But I heard no footsteps.

He knocked me to the ground. "Have you been wasting my time?"

I got up and then stomped toward Nelson Street. It could have been any street; it didn't matter where I was stomping to, just away.

We lived in hotels until I was eighteen. I never did buy new luggage. We moved into a brand-new condo building in the Fairview Slopes neighbourhood, ten minutes from the business district over the Cambie Street Bridge. We were the first tenants. I loved having my own place, not having to pay for it at a reception desk each night. Avery hung his suits in the closet, lined his cologne bottles against his bathroom mirror, making the house a home even as he was still shuttling back and forth between the hotel rooms of my wives-in-law. I had my own bathroom, off the bedroom, and ideas about how I wanted to decorate: I'd start with an Asian motif—lacquered screens, teak chests, medicine cabinets with many drawers.

During that summer we scoured flea markets, warehouse furniture outlets, home electronics stores. Only many years later would I realize the value I'd come to place on these excursions together. Couples bought living room sets when they intended to spend their lives together. No one bought a new bed if their relationship wasn't going to last.

We set the black leather couch diagonally against the corner of the room where it contrasted with the white walls. I put a brass magazine holder at one end of the couch and a brass planter stand holding a marble ashtray at the other. Against one wall I'd arranged a torchiere lamp, a Kenwood stereo, and a six-foot potted palm. Three square windows on the south-facing wall had small plants in each, silhouetted by sunbeams. On the spotless grey carpet was a mirrored coffee table anchored in its precise centre by a vase the colour of jade.

We began taking biannual trips to visit my family on Vancouver Island, catching a ferry to Victoria in the morning and returning that night. My parents and I hadn't reconciled so much as declared an uneasy truce: we spoke of nothing that "mattered." And the occasions when I chose to visit—my birthday, Christmas, cheery occasions in the first place—helped keep the mood light and upbeat. Avery would bond with my father and charm my mother, who would laugh at his jokes. Neither of them knew, of course, what truly lay between Avery and me.

PART II

TEA OF OBLIVION

Realm of the Dead

The Greek word *enantiodromia* refers to the way things change—the tendency for night to become day, for everything, given enough time, to turn into its opposite.

One night I had a bad date, no more or less violent than others I'd had before, and I went home thinking no more about it. Back at the condo there was no sign of Avery. Fine, I'd take a bath; I wanted one anyway, with lots of bubbles, nice and relaxing, and candles on the edge of the tub. I ran the water and had begun undressing when tremors started to rack me.

The man's face had, without warning, jumped back into my head as the bathwater was running. Panicked, I checked the lock on the front door. Then, running on instinct, I stopped the bath, pulled the coffee table into the hall and pushed it against the door, rolling the stereo there too, thinking it would help block the entrance even though it was on wheels. My thinking was primal.

I was trying to barricade myself, convinced the bad date was en route to find me.

The panic slowly subsided along with the bath bubbles. But it didn't disappear entirely.

Over the coming weeks it reared its head anywhere and everywhere, often when I least expected it—while brushing my teeth, measuring coffee into the machine, in a deli with a bag of pierogies in my hand. I'd begun to dread going to work with an intensity I'd never felt before, my fear of being killed the outcome of an unlived life.

Out of the blue I thought, I'll be dead one day.

The absurdity of this, of the phrase itself—*Be* dead? The two states were mutually exclusive—would knock the wind out of me. Life had no purpose. Existence meant nothing in a world where I could lose six friends in a year.

Two had been murdered, one had OD'd, one had shot himself, and two had been diagnosed with AIDS. Those two weren't dead yet, but in 1989 all we knew about AIDS was that it killed. Up until then I'd managed to banish my fear of violent dates, of becoming HIV-positive, through my alter ego. Whose name was Michelle, my street name.

Michelle shared my personal work ethic, but unlike me she didn't dwell on things. Not death. She told me I overanalyzed. According to Michelle, there was no time for reflection, only for fighting.

She robbed dates, she upsold them, she took advantage anywhere she could. She was ruthless, calculating, and frighteningly efficient. She was tougher than me, and in that vein more willing to accept the things I feared—arrest, disease, violence, murder— for the sake of love.

It didn't matter to Avery whether I received a criminal record; he viewed arrests as part and parcel of the trade. The last time I'd been arrested I'd even been sentenced to therapy by the court, but Avery cared as little about my sentence as he did about my tough, violent dates.

Avery saw women as stepping stones; Michelle saw men as tools; both measured people by their munificence. Avery manipulated Suko's overprizing of love, and Michelle manipulated tricks' loneliness; both played people's hopes for profit.

Suko knew tricks weren't worth the intensity of her hatred, but in her fear of losing Avery, she allowed Michelle, like a mistreated hound, to protect her owner.

I directed my anger toward cab drivers, cashiers, waiters— anyone but Avery. I never questioned our relationship; I never wondered whether we belonged together. We *were* together, as if married by custom or arrangement. The question wasn't why but how we'd make what we had work. That's what Michelle said.

Later that week Avery came into the bedroom while I was folding laundry. He moved aside a pile of clothes and sat down on the bed. "I need to tell you something." He turned to me and clasped my fingers in his palms. "I love you. Do you believe me?"

Why was he telling me this? What had he done? It had grown dark outside, murky dusk and parking lot lights. The signal that I'd have to go to work soon.

"I love you, Suko. I really mean it. But. I got to tell you . . . Don't get mad."

Here it comes, I thought.

"A girl chose me last night."

I closed my eyes. *Not again, not again, not again.* Who did I have to share my man with now?

"She chose with fifteen hundred dollars." He handed me his money clip with its wad of fifties and hundreds. "What was I supposed to say, baby? No?"

I flung the money to the floor like a snake. "That's exactly what you say."

Avery left the money where it had landed and bent down to wrap his arms around my knees. "I love you. Because you're not a loser. Like me. The only way I'm getting anywhere is with a woman like you. You know that, don't you?"

I yanked my knees out of his grasp. "You *are* a loser. It's why we're renting a condo and don't own a house."

"I thought you liked this place."

"I'm not talking about that. I'm talking about getting *ahead*. Like, we don't even have a bank account."

The point wasn't the house or the bank account but the effort of keeping my eyes directed ahead, on the prize, despite the dawning awareness that I might never retire.

That night, I knew one thing to be true: if I continued to put on my makeup, my stockings, go to work, buy condoms, I'd be a hypocrite.

Avery was still standing there, his money clip on the carpet, staring at me.

"Is it Cassie?" I asked. Cassie was a friend of his who'd recently come out West. I wasn't supposed to be jealous, even when they spent whole days together, because she wasn't a ho.

"Why would you say something like that?"

I rolled my eyes.

Bam. His open hand had struck my face.

"Don't you ever," he said, "roll your eyes at me."

My face stung. I opened and closed my mouth, not even looking at him.

I drifted away while Michelle resumed folding clothes. Folding and folding, as if packing for a long journey. I had only to step out that door.

The day I found out I was pregnant we were in the Happy Café, a bad name for a place whose carpet, tables, booths were so dingy. Vancouver rain outside the window.

"You look sick," Frances said, her face a mixture of motherly concern and intrigue. Two years from now she'll go missing, and I'll never hear from her again.

Avery lit a cigarette and I pressed my forehead to the window. The cars, the rushing people, made my stomach roll. I fought back nausea. "I feel like crap."

Frances snapped her fingers. "Pregnant," she said. "I'll bet you're pregnant."

I looked down at my underdone sausages, eggs over easy, hash browns, white toast. Mistake. I shifted my gaze to my worn shoes, slanted at the heel, the leather pavement-scuffed.

Finally I pushed my plate away, threw down my fork. "I'm going to throw up."

In the bathroom I stood over a toilet bowl. Rust stains flitted in and out of focus. I steadied myself by putting my hands on the rim of the seat, the black plastic cool against my fingers. The cubicle turned a seaweed colour.

Five minutes later I rinsed my mouth under the tap and returned to the table.

———

The clinic was only a few blocks from the track, but I'd never been inside. I wasn't thinking of a baby at this point. I was thinking of the way strangers on the street would stop a mother to chat, to look into the stroller. Girls I knew from the track who'd gotten pregnant had given their babies names like Gemini or Maximilian or Julius. They took pictures of them with fourteen-carat gold knuckle dusters or surrounded by hundred-dollar bills or sitting atop a fur coat. Could I honestly do the job, be a real mother? It wasn't that I liked the idea of fixing bottles or changing diapers or rocking a little football-sized thing to sleep, but the idea of something between me and Avery as unique as a human being warmed me inside.

I took a urine test and then waited for the result, wondering what kind of parents Avery and I might make. The test confirmed what my body knew.

They called in a counsellor. I felt trapped by the small room, in a chair opposite the woman, a table separating us. I twisted my hands in my lap. What part of the procedure was this?

As she talked I looked out the window and thought about how I would tell Avery I was pregnant. Whether I would tell him at all.

He must want a baby; otherwise, why have sex without a condom?

I thought of Frances, her pregnancies, and knew the answer had nothing to do with babies. Pimps didn't wear condoms. The idea was outrageous. *Who did we think they were, tricks?*

The street nurses had said two girls had been diagnosed with HIV. They'd caught the virus, not at work, where they were meticulous about safe sex, but from their men.

Before I left the clinic the counsellor suggested I write myself a note. "Make a list of the reasons you're getting the abortion," she said. "Put it in an envelope with your name on it, and seal it. Keep it for yourself, for the future."

She'd assumed that's what I wanted: to get rid of the baby.

I nodded my head.

As soon as I unlocked the door to our condo, a prickly rush of anxiety washed over me. This had been happening more and more these days. I lit a joint and smoked it, lying on the carpet. More relaxed, I flipped open a pad of yellow paper and grabbed a pencil. The pages had warranties and receipts stapled into tidy columns next to "Notes to Self" and "Goals in Life" and "Earnings" and "Expenditures." I loved lists. While turning tricks I'd make mental lists of all the movies I'd seen and all the ones I wanted to see. Lists of the colours of sweaters I owned. Lists of favourite songs.

On a clean sheet I drew a white-tailed deer, copying it from a photograph in a magazine lying open beside me. I was stalling.

Writing had been a favourite subject of mine in high school. Solitude had always inspired my creativity. But now, when I turned from the deer drawing to a new yellow page, its blankness swallowed any notion of words. I took another drag and turned back to the deer, adding shading to the hard black lines.

Deep down I knew what the counsellor took for granted: a working girl like me had no choice, only reasons. Moreover, they did not have to be poetry.

I went back to the blank page. Inhaling sharply, I wrote: "I am getting an abortion because of the baby shower."

A ho had gotten pregnant for a pimp who was black. Everyone went to her baby shower. But when the child was born it was white, as white as she was blonde. Everyone stared.

"His skin will darken up," the mother had said, as if convincing herself. "They all start out pale."

But the worry was clear in her face. We turned away in shame. Maybe a condom had burst or slipped off. Maybe she was the kind of ho that didn't give fake lays, maybe she hadn't used a condom at all, was *that* kind of nasty ho that let a trick come inside her for money.

Next I wrote: "Because I had sex with Delbert."

Delbert had been a one-night fling. I hadn't particularly wanted a fling. A couple of months earlier, while we were still living at the Century Plaza Hotel, I came home one night to find that management had double-locked our door: Avery had spent our rent money on crack. I couldn't get hold of him, and I had nowhere else to go.

Not knowing what else to do I went down to the hotel bar, which was full of handsome men; only two were black, so I sat with them. Delbert wasn't handsome but he had a beautiful body and an apartment where I could spend the night. I had sex with him in exchange, I thought, for his hospitality. I didn't expect the anger I felt later. All I could think of was the night Pat and his brother had tried to force themselves on me. The fact that then, too, I'd had nowhere else to go.

I wrote that the news of the baby was the real world colliding with my pretend perfect life with Avery. The one where I pushed a designer stroller down a picket-lined street. Then I wrote that the news was also, ironically, its exact opposite: having the baby was the reality of ending up on a trashy TV show like *Montel*. A teenage prostitute and her pimp.

I put my list in an envelope and sealed it. I printed my full name on the front and placed the envelope in a tote bag filled with pens that had no ink, stuffed-animal key chains, half-used lipsticks, introductory offers for products I didn't need but saved anyway, and two Christmas cards signed by all the street nurses. I replaced the bag under the bathroom sink.

That night I woke up with the bedsheet bunched in my hands. I'd dreamed I'd snatched a baby away from a kidnapper and escaped into a forest. But I'd discovered there was nowhere to hide—the groves had been thinned and were as sun-dappled as a Robert Bateman painting from the mall.

At breakfast I told Avery. Any fantasies of motherhood were crushed into the ground at the precise moment when I said "I'm pregnant" out loud.

I wanted to have a baby for all the wrong reasons. I believed it would make our family more solid, give me comfort. In having a baby to love, I'd be lovable. The transformation from worthless to holy would occur through osmosis.

I can't remember Avery's exact reply. When I told him I'd been to the doctor, that there was no doubt, I imagine he said something like "Wow, shitty," or, with a smile, "Sucks to be you," or, bluntly, "When you getting the abortion?" But it wasn't only the fact that he didn't want the responsibility of parenthood. It was that he didn't want to be a father to *my* baby, get pregnant *with me.* How did I know that?

Because he had a son. So people said. The mother, Maria, happened to be in the lobby of our hotel one night, when we still lived at the Robsonstrasse. She was with her son, Avery's son. Jeremy was about four or five. I couldn't see the resemblance and thought, She's lying about that kid being his. He ran up to Avery and encircled his legs with his arms, saying, "Daddy, Daddy." Avery froze. Looked down at the boy as if he were watching a parasitic worm trying to enter him through his flesh. Glared at Maria, who I knew from the track, who had a reputation for mouthiness. The cleaning ladies in the lobby began to cry. I crumbled. Little pieces of myself broke and fell like shards of ice.

Either shortly before or after this incident, Avery confessed that he'd given Maria money for an abortion as soon as they found out about her pregnancy. She'd left town, gone to Calgary, and claimed that once there she'd booked herself in for a D&C. He discovered her lie only a few years later, when financial documents outlining the money he owed in child support came in the mail. The sum was small, a hundred dollars a month. But it had added up to thousands over time.

Each time I thought of the boy my skin crawled. I railed about a corrupt system that would force Avery to pay arrears, skim any legal earnings or tax returns, dip into his bank account to compensate the mother—when she'd tricked him! Wasn't the onus on *her* to raise the kid without Avery's support? Blackmail. It was as bad as that.

The abortion implied that I was cleverer than Maria, faithful. I'd never play head games. Never mind she was a ho like me and didn't need Avery's money. Unlike her, I'd never sign any piece of paper that authorized officials to put him in jail for being a deadbeat dad. There was no such thing. Only mothers who pushed men into taking on responsibilities they'd never asked for. Who sanctimoniously preached for the right to give birth to an unwanted child. Who, having loudly claimed this right, would run back to a man like a dog with its tail tucked between its legs, needing help. This is what asking for child support was. This is what asking for paternal acknowledgment was. A weak return.

Looking back today, I think it was a self-imposed sense of responsibility that influenced my decision as much as Avery did. Despite what I did for a living, I thought of myself as mature and stable, a dutiful eighteen-year-old who had everything together. The barefoot-and-pregnant-teen stereotype would crash up against that idealized self-image; it would destroy me and fuck up an innocent child in the process.

Besides, it wasn't a child yet. Wasn't even an infant. If I tried hard enough I could convince myself that I had a tumour, not a baby clinging to me for life . . .

The image of Avery's son hugging him in the lobby lodged itself inside me like the fetus. What parent could stand to watch their child reach out for affection only to be pried off as thoughtlessly as a man scrapes barnacles from his boat?

The later revelation was that this image in my head would persist. There was no way of erasing it. No way it would join the ranks of forgotten things.

To stay with Avery would be to remain childless forever. To give up my dream of raising a large family. A huge family—seven, eight, eleven kids, pit bulls and Rottweilers, tomcats, budgies, goldfish, guitars, sunny porches, the door always open. A pot on the stove day and night for anyone who came by. Who hungered. Who knew that, at my house, any comer would find nourishment. Love.

With my hair in pigtails and only lip balm for makeup, wind whistling up my baggy shorts, the street nurse—the one who'd agreed to go with me—didn't recognize me. The one who came to the track every evening, handed out condoms and KY packages that looked like single-serving packets of ketchup, and had just spent eight months in Veracruz. As we left the parking lot and drove along Cambie Street I told myself to calm down, the nurse was with me, nothing bad would happen.

In the waiting room a woman and her mother wore saris that seemed warmer than my own shorts and T-shirt. I shivered and looked to my left. Another family, with a young woman in a mint-green jogging suit, spoke a language I didn't understand. I flipped through a pile of out-of-date women's magazines and then turned to the nurse. "Hey. Thanks for bringing me."

Fifteen minutes passed, then a woman in scrubs called my name. Nothing to it, I told myself. One foot in front of the other. I gave the street nurse a last look and followed the woman in scrubs.

As the anaesthetic made me drift off I thought about the note I'd written, reminding myself of all the reasons why what I was doing was the right thing.

When I'd recovered enough to figure out where I was, I asked for my clothes and got dressed. The street nurse was gone. Still groggy, I laced up my canvas sneakers and went to leave the hospital.

"You have to have someone come and pick you up," a nurse said.

"But why? I live only two blocks away," I lied.

"We can't release you unless you have someone come and pick you up."

"Like who, my boyfriend?"

I knew no one was coming for me.

"Sorry." She rubbed her angular forehead. She truly did look sorry. "It's policy."

I looked her in the eye and tried to imagine how she thought she'd keep me here. What would she do if I popped her one on the chin right now? Flattened her against the wall, kicking her to the floor?

And why wasn't Avery with me in the first place?

I marched to a pay phone and called my drug dealer, Debra. She used to have a different name. Then she went to a nameologist to find out why she was having such bad luck in her life, why her relationship with the owner of an auto body shop was disintegrating after fifteen years, why she couldn't find a decent apartment in the West End for less than twelve hundred a month. He told her, *Change your name to Debra.* I was calling her partly because I had no inkling where Avery was and partly because the thought that he might say he was too busy to come was too much to bear.

We lived in the condo in Fairview Slopes for three years. Then, when I was about to turn twenty-one, we moved into a rented house in a suburban neighbourhood on the outskirts of Vancouver known as Burquitlam. This was a move up. To distance oneself from where one plied one's trade, to have more property, more square footage—these things represented evolution. Progress.

Some memories arrive unbidden like packages in the post, waiting to be opened. Others come to me like whispers from another room, half-recalled phrases, a stance, an inflection, muted by drugs and time. From these remnants I reconstruct a conversation held on the track. The details I don't remember.

What comes back to me is a woman named Tanya. Blond and bubbly, she had the face of a high school cheerleader. But my impression of her townhouse near the Vancouver–Burnaby border, the rundown banality of it, evoked the question: "Why bother working the track if this is where you live?"

As we must have on other days, we strolled around the track, "doing a loop." The high school equivalent of doing a loop—half designed to increase your visibility, half to show off to the other hos who your friends were—would be deciding whether to sit with the in-crowd or the losers at lunch.

I was younger than Tanya but made more money, dressed better, and never drank at work.

The memory takes place in daylight, so I must have been working afternoon shifts, reckoning with either a police curfew or a red zone.

At some point in the conversation, Tanya revealed she'd slept with Avery. She compared who he was then, years ago, to who he was now.

"Crack bumps," she said. The drug-induced cysts on his face.

I wasn't jealous or threatened, even when she winked and said he "did things," like go down on her. The part of the conversation that made an impression was how she believed he'd slid downhill since then.

I'm making this up. I must have overheard her talking to another ho, because I can't invent the circumstances that would have made her badmouth Avery to my face.

"He used to be fine," she said, "but he's not anymore."

Her remark didn't insult. Instead, a deep relief washed away the fear I'd been carrying inside: that every ho wanted to get with my man.

Over time I'd run off, or outlasted, all the rest. I'd had no wives-in-law for a while.

My staying power, the obedience I showed to my pimp, otherwise known as being down, had earned me respect and a reputation for being solid.

"Look at what Michelle goes through," a pimp once told his ho when she was complaining about his treatment. "At least you're not Michelle." The horrors I was believed to endure were to me no more than quotidian aspects of The Game—bringing home a large trap, never talking back—but hearing that had renewed my sense of pride.

Now, hearing Tanya describe Avery's deterioration made me pity him.

"Base head," I think she said.

But he was my base head.

I was the only one now. Avery was too old, too washed up, to attract anyone new. That this made me want to treat him with a new tenderness tells me about who I was then.

To be so pleased that I was the last of the many good hos Avery had had in his ten-year pimping career, to be so pleased with being left with the dregs—that tells me I wanted to be viewed as a martyr.

Leftovers were my privilege. The injury crack had done to his reputation solidified our relationship; it made him dependent on me.

To be down gave me a sense of power. In a counterintuitive way, my obedience to a man who in the eyes of other hos no longer deserved it, or commanded it, my ability to put that onus of high performance on myself, fuelled a self-righteous streak.

That night, I told Avery nothing of what Tanya had said. Perhaps I mentioned that I'd chatted with someone he knew. If I mentioned her name perhaps he said "Who?" not to spare me jealousy, but the crack having made him forget, gratifying me further.

I reduced him to a little boy whom I had to protect. I didn't think, Hey, other hos consider your man a loser. Maybe it's time you abandoned ship.

Instead I grew secure in the knowledge that I'd never have to deal with another wife-in-law again. Avery had lost his game. His looks. His status. In the years we'd spent together he'd let himself go to the point where his only choice remaining was to rely on me alone. And I was happy, privileged, to comply.

I'd take care of him. I'd make everything okay.

I'd be such a good ho he'd never miss his stable.

Avery must have intuited the truth. It hadn't occurred to me till then that his nighttime forays no longer involved elaborate preparations. The clothes, the hair, the meticulously detailed car.

Now he ventured out in tracksuits, without even showering first. His hair in a ponytail.

Avery had become a monogamous boyfriend. We lived common-law, introducing each other as "my partner" in public.

Yet even as these things were taking place, Avery and I had begun to drift apart, spending more time on solitary pursuits—I on my writing and he on his car collection, to which he'd recently added a '71 Chevelle SS he was in the process of restoring. We shared the new house like two strangers, polite but distant, tolerating each other's presence.

The Hong Kong developer who owned our house didn't do much to maintain it. No repairs had been done since we'd moved in. The rotten porch steps barely held a person's weight and the fridge ran warm, souring milk in two days. Still, our new endeavour benefited from a negligent overseas landlord: we'd decided to start a grow op.

Frances was the only person I would have told about it—about how, before I went to work at night, I'd go down to the basement where we kept our three hundred plants. Naked in grow-light heat, I'd pluck dead leaves and wipe away spider mites. I loved the pungency of the foliage, my fingers in dirt. I loved the geometry of the plants, the precision and perfection of their rows. I loved how our neighbour made hash oil out of the trimmings we threw over the fence.

One rainy evening, searching for writing magazines, I drove down slick streets to a bookshop on West Fourth. The woman there gave me a magazine with glossy pages that told you how to write articles, how to dissect stories, where to submit your work.

I sent three poems to *Quarry* magazine and a few months later received a handwritten rejection letter from one of its editors, with a note on how to subscribe and a free copy of their twentieth-anniversary issue. I opened its pages. My eye fell on Caroline Adderson's short story, "Oil and Dread." I'd not been discovered, but I was discovering something. I saw at once that these words were different from any I'd read before. The rhythm like a river, dappled currents of lyricism.

The story stayed with me as I tended to the plants that night. I kept thinking about the mystery and power of its language. It made me shudder, like a girl falling in love.

I'd crunched numbers and pointed out to Avery that the grow op made enough money to sustain us. At age twenty-one I was working the streets less now than ever before. For the first time in my life I had a home office.

And for the first time I became disciplined, fastidious about my writing. I worked for four hours a day and in the evenings I'd read for four hours, keeping tally in a scribbler: how much was fiction, how much nonfiction. I adhered to my routine as if clinging to a life raft.

Even as I was still going to work three or four nights a week, I was cultivating a new self. Literature was my communion. One day I'd make magic with my words.

Town of Quitters

By the summer of 1992 what lay between Avery and me was no longer love but a deep and narrow crevasse filled with resentments. We kept drifting further apart, I into my writing, he "out with the boys" for days at a time. I'd phone the jails, the hospitals, then awake to a loud knock on the door at three a.m. "Where's your man? I need to speak to him very, very badly." When I'd confront him the one thing that had changed was his attitude. No trace of bombast remained, only guilt and remorse on a sweaty face he'd lower into his hands. Eyes that looked up at me, minutes later, when he dared meet my gaze, filled with tears.

By October we'd saved enough money to go on vacation in Mexico. The preparations alone excited me: the reading of maps, fingers hovering over exotic place names. I loved that first trip. I loved how much more real everything felt without razors and makeup and hair extensions and stilettos. I hiked until the sweat ran in rivulets down my dirty face, streaking it like mascara. And over the six weeks we travelled, Avery stayed away from the crack pipe. We did nothing more than smoke Mexican red hair joints and drink our faces off.

I admired his ability to make friends, to break the ice, to get a room laughing, to turn a ho-hum night into a party. A couple of lawyers from Seattle staying in Tulum asked me, "Is he always like this?"

"Yup," I said, and it was true. Like a little boy, Avery was either happy or mad. There was no in between.

He was my buffer. My link to the outside.

My identity had been subsumed by his for so long that I didn't know how to be on my own. Travelling gave me the chance to discover who I was. We define ourselves in the context of others. Surrounded by young professionals, I met in myself someone new. We befriended an interracial couple from the Netherlands, a literary magazine editor from Belgium and his wife, a German man in his last year of med school. He was in his twenties. Not much older than me.

My personality snuck out like a woman's slip from beneath a dress. I left it like that, to see other people's reactions.

I romanticized the shirts of childrens' school uniforms in front of dirt floor shacks encircled by barbed wire. In a country where dogs ran loose in packs, poverty wasn't a vice, not a character flaw. Poverty did not equal weakness or my father's failure as a man; oversimplifying the equation, I began viewing poverty as an ingredient for happiness. And freedom.

Like someone falling in love, I idealised the reek of open sewers, and piles of used diapers in the river and plastic bags in the mango trees. Two months we travelled and smog, even dead dogs, became symbols of virtue. The Mexico I saw was one where I walked with wild hair and shoeless feet, sun scorching off my inauthenticity, the juice of a golden pineapple dripping from my chin not caring who saw, singing with the hurdy gurdy players on street corners. A place of sweetness. A place of reggaeton music. A place without disguise.

I'd always reflected the person Avery wanted me to be. It never occurred to me that this was a process. In the pursuit of love, I'd let him mould me. The best I could hope for was that his desires would evolve, that through his evolution he'd learn to bring out the best in me.

In other words, clay had better hope its sculptor is skilled. That his vision for what it can become is not only excellent but that his hands are talented enough to bring that vision to fruition.

But my sense-of-things permeated a question I often asked myself: Who would I be now if I'd chosen someone besides Avery? I could as easily have ended up with the type of man I'd heard horror stories about: who beat his hos with clothes hangers or cut out their tongues for talking back.

We returned from Mexico vowing to travel at least every two years. As with so much else, it never happened.

I'd been a smoker since I was eleven years old. I'd often tell people, "If I ever want to quit, they're going to have to lock me in a room alone. Because when I'm nicking out I could kill someone." Quitting meant that rawness in your body, nerve endings exposed.

I'd gone so far as to record how often I smoked each day in a notebook I carried in my back pocket. The idea was that before quitting you should shake up the foundations on which the addiction rested, first by recording and then by analyzing the data: what things prompted the need to light up. Then you could retrain yourself by choosing to smoke at longer and longer intervals.

With diligence, I managed to cut down so that, unless the track had been stressful, I no longer had days where I smoked two packs or more.

Controlling my smoking at work was impossible. My pattern had always been to light up as soon as I got into a cab with a date, then again at the hotel room, then again when the trick had finished. A violent date meant I chain-smoked. Lighting a cigarette gave me time to invent a response to a dangerous situation.

But when we got back from vacation, I quit. Cold turkey. How? In my mind, the equation looked like this: if you don't smoke, you can retire. If you can cut your expenses to the degree that cigarettes are no longer a daily purchase, you can stay home. As I eased into not-working, day by day, the last thing I wanted was Avery saying, "You got to go back to work. How're you going to afford smokes otherwise?" In my mind, the two were uniquely and absolutely related. If I could keep the cigarettes away from my lips, I'd never have to suck another cock for money again. Never have to stand in the rain waiting to break, my feet getting soaked through my leather stilettos. Never have to deal with another bad date—as I had the night before we'd left for Mexico.

He hadn't been satisfied with my performance, especially after giving me an added couple hundred dollars on top of the one-fifty he'd already spent. He yelled at me. I couldn't get out of the room; he was blocking the door. My body began twitching like a live wire. Even as it was happening I felt embarrassed by what it revealed about me—that I was scared. Always a terrible thing before a showdown. I tried to control my body by sitting down on the bed and calmly lighting a smoke, exhaling in a relaxed fashion, a ruse to let him know he didn't intimidate me. What saved me wasn't the cigarette but another working girl who burst into the room. She'd heard his shouts.

Her tactic was to call direct attention to my fear.

"Look at her," she said. "She's frightened. What have you done? You, this big man, and her, scared half to death."

As she talked I inched closer to her, toward the door, and both of us edged ourselves past him and out into the hallway.

I smoked the rest of my Mexican cigarettes when we got home.

Returning to the track right away seemed unreasonable. I had laundry to do, souvenirs to unpack—a friend had looked after our plants while we were gone but there was a crop ready to harvest, to trim. The track would have to wait.

But what if, what if I cost hardly anything to keep? If I never bought another stitch of clothing? If I never smoked again? If there was nothing Avery could throw in my face?

I'd set it up as though one action caused the other, as if smoking triggered turning tricks. I'm astounded by my power to delude myself into making the oddest connections. My theory that quitting smoking meant I could square up made no sense. But at the time the formula seemed foolproof. And in the manner of cultures whose stories aren't spoken for fear of draining their power, I said nothing to Avery about my plan. I told him only that I wasn't going to smoke anymore, not why. The key element was the why: that this endeavour's success or failure would change the course of my life. My identity.

I no longer wanted to be two people, Michelle on the track, and Suko at home.

I wanted to be me all the time. I wanted care about the people I met enough to remember their names.

Every time I wanted a cigarette I lit a joint instead. Then I'd put it out, stare out the window at the traffic rolling down Ingersoll Street, and think, How badly do you not want to go back to the track?

If not smoking meant that every day could be danger-free, that evenings could be as blank a page as my mornings and afternoons, to be filled with books, writing, tending the plants, watching *Star Trek* . . . then the cravings would become manageable.

The new perspective I'd gained from travelling showed me, showed both of us, that the world and what it could offer was bigger than the track, bigger than a grow op, bigger than we could imagine.

Once a week at the library downtown I'd read the bulletin board that advertised upcoming contests and editorial services. I read how-to-write books and magazines like *Quarry*. And the more stories I read, the more I fantasized about leaving Avery.

(In years to come we'll be standing in a kitchen. I'll lean against the counter of a house I don't live in while Avery slugs from a bottle of rye. Smoking crack all night has made him chatty. As the sun rises he tells me that all the times he said he was going out with the boys, he was smoking crack. He seems excited to reveal this information to me, his voice rushing and cheerful. "I could have cheated on you," he says, "a lot more than I did." In this dynamic there's no judgment or anger, only a shared crack pipe and a bottle we both raise to our lips.)

I began to see myself walking out the door, renting a housekeeping room, saving for travel. But other days, leaving the world I'd known for years seemed unfathomable, amounted to an admission of failure.

I joined a choir; no audition required, simply a desire to sing. Once a week I'd catch two buses and the SkyTrain into town. The Rainbow Choir was made up of a New Agey collection of mostly women. The one who led it called herself Julie Blue and wrote songs about dolphins and talking trees. One evening, in an exercise designed to expand intimacy among the group, Julie Blue passed out little stones from a fabric bag she wore around her neck.

I put the stone in my mouth while I cooked dinner or scrubbed the toilet. Small and grey, the rest of the time it sat in my office. When I wrote I held it in my hand.

I signed out new self-help books, with titles along the lines of *The Art of Letting Go* and *How to Forgive*.

Trying to write my way out felt like turning off one light while turning on another.

We had a shared history. We remembered the same parties, the same people. But Avery was no longer the man of my dreams.

We'd managed to keep things afloat. Our ventures had been profitable. We owned a Mustang, a Corvette, a Cougar speedboat, a Chevelle, and a van for our "auto glass business."

Avery had run a company in Alberta, a shop he'd started with a friend involving auto glass. At least, I thought it did—they may have also done body work. The salient part of the story, though, was the fact that they'd taken out a thirty thousand dollar loan to make their dream come true. Avery was in his early twenties at the time and had gotten out of jail after a two-years-less-a-day stint for assault.

But after a year, the friend drained the bank account and ran off, leaving Avery holding the bag. As a result—with warrants out for his arrest in Alberta—he fled the country with what cash remained in the till. The warrants were provincial, meaning he couldn't be shipped back to the land of oil and cowboy hats to do time.

We went to a bookstore and bought a how-to guide. Everything we needed to know to fill out the paperwork was contained within its pages. The book even gave tips on naming one's business. We decided on Arrow Mobile Auto Glass, since beginning with A meant it would be one of the first things people would see in the phone book. I spent hours filling out forms, crossing t's and dotting i's. Our application for a licence was successful; it came in the mail, an official piece of paper that I put into a briefcase. We opened a business account. We had signs made up for our van, the same van we used for the bags of soil our pot plants grew in. The signs were magnetic, and so could be easily removed if we wanted. We designed a logo for the business: "Arrow" spelled out inside an actual arrow, two feet by three feet and coloured white, red, and black. We made up a slogan—"We move so you don't have to"—and printed it as a tagline on the bottom of the signs, under the arrow. The professional-looking van signalled to people who drove past our house that responsible adults lived there.

I breezed through paperwork, the formulas needed to pay taxes at intervals throughout the year. I was hopeful that this process represented a shift in Avery's outlook toward a view that was more in line with mine: namely, that we'd finally go legit. I no longer wanted to live looking over my shoulder. I wanted to pay taxes, something I'd never done before. To be the kind of person who paid taxes. I no longer wanted to live in fear that an official from Revenue Canada was going to knock on our door, point at all the material goods we'd amassed, the speedboat, the cars, the leather furniture, my camera equipment, and say, "Where'd all this stuff come from? Unless you can prove it was obtained legally, we're going to seize it all. You owe us." I was terrified of being audited, of the government seizing and then auctioning off what we'd worked hard for. Arguing with an imaginary bureaucrat, I'd defend my position. "Where the hell were you when I needed you? I never asked you for anything and now you want to rip everything away from me?"

My defensive posturing hid the fact that I longed to be the kind of adult who contributed to society, who understood that tax dollars make the country's social safety net possible.

Sifting through paperwork took time, but the math wasn't difficult; it was within my capabilities.

I thought of ways we could advertise, how we could get Avery more business than the trickle of phone calls from friends wanting a good deal for removing a chipped windshield, a cracked passenger window.

For the duration of my relationship with Avery, the pinnacle to reach had always been the "one day" when we'd have our own business. Another ho and her man had bought a laundromat. I felt optimistic that this move toward legitimacy represented progress in our evolution as human beings.

We caught a ferry to one of the Gulf Islands so that Avery could change a windshield for a man who'd gotten his number through friends. I watched more than helped as he removed the old windshield and put in a new one we'd brought over in the van, held securely on the boat voyage in a custom rack he'd built that could hold up to seven windshields at a time. In a driveway surrounded by tall evergreens, carpeted with pine needles and cones, he lowered the windshield with rope, craftily slipping it into the rubber seal that would hold the glass in place; then he pulled the rope away by degrees so that the windshield sank into the empty space in the seal he'd already filled with glue. His arms flexed, his hands got dirty.

Looking back now, I think Avery went along with the plan so he could say "See, I wasn't lying. After all these years, we've got our business." He never intended to expand it past the point of frivolity; for him it was consequential only as a front for the weed-growing operation. Filling out chits for ICBC, the province's insurance program, felt like a game. Our money came from weed; plus, our Mobile Arrow company allowed us to write fake receipts for services never performed. So, while Avery ignored calls from potential customers, we'd deposit the grow op's profits into the Arrow account.

Nonetheless, I'd proven to myself that I was smart enough to run a business. I had the means to organize as well as the skills to seek out the information I needed to make things happen.

And I'd stopped working the streets. I can mark down the date on a calendar but there was no declaration, no singular point in time where I identified as a working girl and then didn't.

Iron Web and Office of Fair Trading

The car pulled in around noon. Even from a distance I'd recognized the rumble of the 454 engine that Avery had installed in the blue Chevelle. Not the stock motor—but then it wasn't even a real Chevelle SS. Like so much about our lives, it was fake. He'd added the racing stripes and the SS chrome himself. As he got out of the car I spoke to him over the fence that divided the carport from the backyard.

"Just getting home?" I said, stating the obvious. The subtext: Why have you stayed out all night? Don't you know I keep track on the calendar? When the x's I've marked outweigh the unmarked dates, a catastrophe will take place.

He grinned the unmistakable grin of someone high. The contortions idiosyncratic to each addict. The grin also held shame.

I'd been awake for hours. So had he, all night by the looks of it.

I continued busying myself with small outdoor tasks, puttering away as if his presence meant nothing to me.

"I don't care, you know."

Still he said nothing. But he didn't make a move to go into the house, either.

Remorse, promises, failures, more promises, begging. How easy for anyone to look at the addict and say, "It's not his fault." I lacked the essential part of the argument: that this didn't mean I had to let it into my own life. Back then, it was too easy to equate leaving because of his drug addiction with being a judgmental person— something I abhorred. To leave because of an illness was mean. What about for better or for worse? In sickness and in health? In these ways and others I'd rationalized his addiction, my staying. I'd chosen to believe him when he said he quit and ignore his nights out as normal.

"You and I," I continued, "have absolutely nothing in common. So, I have a plan. How's about you live your life and I live mine. We'll keep them separate. Like meat and potatoes on a plate."

His demeanour crumpled. "But I don't want that," he said. "I don't want you to live your own life."

"If you didn't know me today, would you still seek me out? I doubt it. In fact, you hate my type."

We both knew it was the truth.

"Nothing," I underlined the word, "in common." I took pleasure in this, in being cruel, fuelled by anger, his duplicity, the strength of my conviction. A wall went up between us. Surrounded by my books, working toward getting my General Equivalency Diploma and practising the writing portion of the test, a three hundred word essay, the only assignment I cared about, I could live with him while knowing that only my body walked around that house.

In a few months his addiction would see the Chevelle and the twenty-five thousand dollars we'd put into its restoration gone— all to cancel out a seven-thousand-dollar drug debt.

Accrued when he partied down the street at a restaurant owned by a friend of his. At first, I'd been relieved that he was hanging with the boys and not in the bar chasing skirts. Avery did nothing but grind his jaw when he got high. He could never fuck a woman.

I released myself from caring about his wants and needs.

The fence between us was perfect. I stepped away, into the sunshine, as if to prove how little this all meant to me—knowing he couldn't follow. I'd spent half the night crying but now stood in the sun. Avery was left in the shade of the carport, which stank exactly like the garbage we kept there. I wasn't weak, and I didn't need him.

I understand now that the burden was never on me to save him. A person can be saved only if you have their permission.

So, with that certain measure of cruelty all ultimatums contain, I walked out with my backpack, leaving a note saying that if he wanted me to return he'd better think about things. Left my car, the note, our dog, and over the dog alone I cried. Sure I'd never return, I waited for a bus that would take me to the West End.

I went to my friend Patti's. I'd met her at a writers' camp in Campbell River where twenty contest winners were sent to workshop under Jack Hodgins, a local writer.

I'd titled my story "Fear." I wrote about living in a biker house, stereo blaring, the coffee table and shot glasses, the empties in the kitchen. I described how it felt to be choked against a wall, how hands squeezing your throat felt from holding your breath. The surprise that a neck could support the weight of your body as easily as it held up your head.

The other participants spoke of Jack Hodgins in hushed tones, or, if addressing him directly, did so with lowered eyes that bordered on awe. I'd never heard of him, nor did I know what a "workshop" was. I'd been horrified to learn, on my first day of the seven-day camp, that *workshop* was a verb. "To workshop" meant that you read everyone else's short story, that you came to class prepared to share your comments out loud. So that's why they sent us an envelope stuffed full of fiction, I thought.

Others characterized my work as "raw." Most of the participants were older. Apart from Patti and me, no one else was in their twenties. One woman, in her thirties, had worked as an editor for *PRISM international* magazine. More than Jack Hodgins, it was she whom I revered. Whom I shyly spoke to. With whom I exchanged phone numbers. Not only because she had beautiful red hair and drove a cool vintage car and sang in a jazz band, but because she'd worked for a magazine where I'd long been sending my work. Whose every issue I read in the Vancouver Public Library as if studying the Bible.

Speaking to Avery on the phone from Patti's apartment, I told him that things had to change.

The trip, I added, was the only thing that would save us.

By now I'd been off the track for four years. Time contracts or expands according to how it fills: routine blurs years; time speeds up walking the dog, taking out the garbage. When settling into a movie before bed could be any other day, time seems reversible, you can move ahead, or backward. In moments of drama, time tightens its chains affixing events to us forever. Adventure marks its irreversibility, yet the days in which nothing happens slip by without leaving a mark.

The years that followed were steady, predictable. I lived inside my stories, fooling myself with words. I grasped at my history, recounting it, and saw yesterday through mine and Avery's stories, negating the present while sucking the past dry. Time flowed with the speed of a river, sweeping me up in a surge of thoughts, occasionally crashing on the rocks of Avery's violence that I had once confused for passion. I rewrote myself.

Even though we'd blown through the half-million dollars I'd earned, he'd granted me equal time to write. I'd worked as his ho for four years. I'd written for four years, without working the track. Now the books were balanced; we were even. Stay or leave, it didn't matter.

He could fund a trip for me, I said to him over the phone, or I'd leave. Furthermore, the trip came with no guarantees. The distance between us gave me leverage. From Patti's living room I could make demands.

We decided to give it one more shot: we'd travel together much as some couples have a baby together to strengthen their bond. Because Avery's sister had said he wouldn't survive without me. Because he said he'd do anything to make it work.

Avery placed an ad for our Mustang in the *Buy & Sell* newspaper, listing it for ten thousand dollars. A few days later the man who'd buy the Mustang, our last remaining car, stood in our living room.

He picked things up, looked at them, and put them back down as if he owned the place.

The week before I'd stood in Patti's living room, tears streaming down my face.

"You know you were right to leave him." She paused. "Right?"

She'd once had a suicidal boyfriend. Whenever they fought he threatened to do himself in. After I stopped crying I asked her what had happened to him. "Did he kill himself?"

"Don't know. Don't care."

Now I watched the man walk around, pompous as a peacock, as Avery answered his questions about the car. I knew his type: gym monkey, too much testosterone. He hadn't spoken to me once or bothered to look my way even though I was by Avery's side the whole time. Finally the man asked for a test drive.

Avery returned a while later with no car and eight thousand dollars cash.

We gave up the house, the dog, the grow op, and put all our furniture into storage. Funding the trip with the proceeds from the Mustang, we left at the beginning of August 1995 for Central America.

I bought a Jack Hodgins book to bring along.

For the next four months Avery danced and made friends with everyone, regardless of where we were. A mountain town in Guatemala where we studied Spanish at a school that had a Homestay program, butchered chickens for dinner, and ate tamales wrapped in corn. On an island in Honduras. In the ruins of Copán. On a beach in Playa del Carmen. Every action brought him closer to an essential version of himself. We swam with sharks and barracuda. Learned how to score pot in Spanish, how to roll it in banana leaf. He was becoming the man he'd always meant to be.

We met a man sailing around the world. My teenage love for boats and the sea resurfaced. "The ocean as your home," I said.

"To make a move like that . . ." I said dreamily to Avery that night. We'd figure out the logistics upon our return. "What do you think?"

"I'm in."

We had no plan; for now, it was enough to know we shared a vision.

When we got back to Vancouver in December, we rented a small apartment off Commercial Drive. I made up index cards with our names and phone number—"Couple happy to crew for food and berth"—and added that I could cook, that Avery could fix anything broken. "Pin them up at yacht clubs," I told Avery. "Find a bulletin board by the Westin." Rather than buy our own sloop, we'd learn how to sail on someone else's first.

But he never pinned up any cards. They lay in a pile on the kitchen counter, where they remained. I refused to move them. I couldn't touch them, much less clear them away. Their presence on the spotless counter spoke of more than I could bear to hear.

I looked out the bedroom window onto a potholed alley lined with dumpsters and the back of another four-storey walk-up like ours, a low-cost housing initiative from the seventies. Four narrow flights of stairs up to our rooms with their mouldy tiles, scored floorboards, wall cracks, mice, cockroaches, bricked-off fireplace, cardboard walls. I saw only death and decay.

I'd been trying to write, but my sense of uncertainty about the future, and about myself, ruined every story I started. I couldn't find the right voice; the apprehension I felt had infected my writing. The answer was clear. No amount of craft or technique would improve me so long as I stayed with Avery.

My great-grandfather, the story goes, abandoned his wife and children for months, even years, at a time. Chased women. Gambled. Through sheer grit his family managed to survive, even thrive, during his absences. But, to my amazement, my great-grandmother would let him return at intervals to collect money from their meagre savings, to reclaim his place as head of the household. How easily beauty blends with ruin.

This story haunts me.

I had to believe there was more to my great-grandmother's compliance than simple weakness or stupidity. I saw myself in her.

On my office wall was what I called my memory box. Wooden with a glass front, it held things from my childhood. Among them was a bookmark I once drew of Alice in Wonderland where she cried so hard that everyone floated away on her tears. Carried off by her sadness, washed away by her pain.

My writing would do this. Wash away my pain.

Vindication. *I write to be free. The words will free me.* Then it would all have been worth it. All? What all? The streets, Avery? Yes, I'd show them. A child's threat: "Then they'll be sorry." For years in my secret heart I'd been waiting for discovery. It felt like reaching in the dark—for an outstretched hand that would touch me, *know* me.

I sat in my office and made myself write lines:

You will not be homeless.
You will not go hungry.
You will continue to write.
You will get your break.
You will make your own money.
You will have the options you have created.

I also wrote a to-do list:

Extract self from all joint accounts and ventures.
Gather precious belongings, snorkel, Christmas cards.
Money!
Call landlord.
Photocopy birth certificate, SIN, passport. Keep in a safe place.
Cut an extra set of house keys and hide them?

Then I wrote a story as if I had five minutes left to live.

But first I needed a way to survive, resources to deal with the repercussions of leaving. I found myself a "socially significant" job working at the Wilderness Committee, an environmental group that lobbied for the protection of old-growth forest. My role as a canvasser was to go door to door Mondays through Thursdays to talk about upcoming campaigns and collect donations. The pay was $120 a week, plus commissions for signing up members.

When I had enough in the bank, I left Avery.

———

January 17, 1996. I woke that morning and pretended to still be asleep. Avery kissed my forehead, his whiskers tickling my face. Then his steel-toed boots were clomping across the hardwood of the living room. He had a new job at a body shop, an effort to prove the sincerity of his love, but I knew better than to think it would last.

As soon as I heard the door click shut I jumped out of bed and started putting things in my backpack: my snorkel, spices, a shoe-box full of negatives of every photo we'd taken in our years together, computer disks of my writing, my teddy bear. When I caught a glimpse of myself in the mirror, my reflection shocked me—I was only twenty-four and suddenly, somehow, I'd grown old. I knew instinctively that this was how I'd look for the rest of my life. But I kept packing, imagining how it would be when Avery came home that night—*if* he came home—and saw my goodbye note on the coffee table.

I caught a whiff of my shirt and felt a stab of pain, realizing that its scent—half the smell of home, half the smell of him—would never be the same again.

All I'd been doing was bursting into tears. I cried in the work van. When I revealed to my boss what was going on in my life, he suggested we take the night off. While the others canvassed their neighbourhoods we sat in a pub and talked.

Now I was in the Swartz Bay ferry terminal. As soon as I saw my father I repeated the performance. Beyond the tears, I felt a renewal. Was it possible that each time I cried it hurt less? Was I getting used to it?

I'd called my parents and told them I was leaving Avery. I must have, though I have no clear recollection of the conversation. My father was waiting for me at the top of the escalator that spit out foot passengers from Vancouver one after another like a row of toy soldiers.

We didn't talk much on the drive home.

The drive home? To their house. Where was home? I'd lost mine. I'd lost my connection to who I was, as represented by the furniture and clothing and knickknacks that we'd collected over the years and that I'd been forced to leave behind. I was twenty-four years old, had a grade nine education, an insubstantial piece of paper that said I had the general equivalent to my grade twelve, and everything I owned fit into a backpack. But I had a bit of money.

I stayed with them for two weeks.

Unlike the earlier time I'd left Avery, staying at Patti's for a few days, this time I'd abandoned Vancouver. Already—with the Georgia Strait separating us—this move felt more permanent. The larger divide meant I wasn't coming "home."

Whenever disagreements had broken out between us Avery would say "Go home to your parents." Now, for the first time ever, I'd done that. I'd never phoned to ask them for anything before. I hadn't lived with them since the age of fifteen. And now, a decade later, they'd taken me in, the prodigal daughter.

Over the days that followed I watched my parents with each other, the way they'd bicker over the smallest things, and I wondered: Was my relationship with Avery so bad?

My parents' house smelled the way I remembered it: food aromas mixed with the lavender my mother grew and which my father wasn't allergic to. I observed him, his collection of quirks, his unchanging rule, and wondered once again: What's wrong with me? My mother has remained married to this person. Why can't I stay with Avery?

This was a lame attempt at self-comfort. To give myself a false cushion to fall asleep on. The hope that tomorrow would bring us back together.

I tried to think of other things. Like the biologist at work who'd asked me to join him for a bike ride.

In the weeks leading up to my leaving Avery, he and I had often slept in separate bedrooms. I could still hear him snoring, but I found myself pretending I was in my own apartment. When I masturbated, I no longer thought about him but about my co-workers. I imagined giving my body to anyone new. How it would feel.

I approached finding a new home with the same sense of curiosity.

The Wilderness Committee had said my job would be waiting for me whenever I returned. And so, after those two weeks with my parents, I planned to leave Victoria the next morning, find a place that afternoon, and be back at work that evening.

When I got back to the city I visited a few rooming houses, including one that accepted only men. Late in the day, I found one on Water Street, right across from where I worked. It charged $375 a month for a room and had security cameras on every floor.

It didn't bother me that I'd have to share a bathroom with the whole floor. I'd approach the experience in the way I'd always wanted to travel: on a shoestring budget, exchanging comfort for adventure.

From the outside I may have seemed directionless, but I knew what I wanted. To get out of the country altogether. And to never come back, as if leaving Canada could transform me into who I was destined to become.

I pinched every penny. I went without food; I washed my clothes and hair and dishes with the bar soap that could be had for fifty cents in Chinatown.

I began smoking again that week. I'd been off cigarettes for three years, but my fear of returning to the track no longer lingered in the drags I inhaled with pleasure, liberated. The idea of turning a trick felt different to me now. I even called a girl I'd once worked with, whose escort ad I'd seen, to ask if she had any spare clients, any doubles she needed help with. Had she said yes I'd have turned a trick in order to leave Canada that much faster.

What I know now, and didn't know then, was that true change comes from that little fire within us. As a trick had once said, "What you're running from is in you."

Back then, though, I still believed that change was wrought from the outside in. Like forest fires, storms, and acid rain, change was an external authority. The key, as I knew it then, was to exercise the same care in choosing my environs as a prospective buyer debating the purchase of a house on a cliff.

Now I know that true change means we're no longer mutable from the outside, staying ourselves no matter what the weather. Less like clay, more like bamboo, swaying, not breaking, in a stiff wind.

Back then, I was trying to cobble myself together out of bits others had thrown away, with a box of mismatched tools.

I'd revoked reminders of my old self. I'd renounced violence. I worked in the perfect environment to politically charge high heels, makeup. In a world where children starved and bombs fell, the vanity of combing one's hair, the patriarchal bondage of close-fitting clothing entrapped others, but not me.

With a gusto reserved for the born-again I stormed the annual general meeting of a large logging corporation. I boycotted McDonald's. I became a vegetarian.

First week of September, 1996. The air had cooled and amid the green leaves a few had turned orange, clinging to branches in the breeze as if there were a point in hanging on. Six months earlier I'd moved into a housekeeping room in Gastown. Now I was about to call Avery from the parkade next door. Cars roared in and out of that cavernous, yellow-lit space, mocking my own stasis. Would he hang up? Or feign friendliness so he could kick my ass? I wanted to believe I was doing well, but my summer alone, the clubs and one-night stands, had been anything but fun. I wanted to tell him how long those months had felt, how I'd crank up reggae in my little room, spinning until laughter and tears made me stop.

What I ended up telling Avery was that old friends had made me think of him. He asked me if I was happy.

What could I say?

I'd always thought happiness was a kind of completion, the circle's end after you'd made your way around. Happiness the byproduct of achievement.

I'd left Avery, started a new life.

Isn't that what I'd wanted?

Why was I miserable? So lonely?

I'd pegged happiness wrong.

Twenty minutes later Avery was hugging me right off the ground, smelling of cologne, wearing a brand-new tracksuit.

Then I saw the rundown East Vancouver house he'd moved into: cockroach infested, bathtub ringed with black grease, laundry basket overflowing, Molson-can crack pipe on the kitchen counter, flats of empty beer cans on the bedroom floor, flies everywhere, mice-chewed pizza boxes piled in corners, a photograph of us at

Playa del Carmen tacked to the wall. I knew what it meant now, that brand-new tracksuit, the cleanliness of his skin. I knew how far he'd come to get me.

The house in East Van wasn't a place to buy a plant and place it on the windowsill, to buy vegetables for dinner, to raise the blinds. It wasn't a place for sunshine, for watching the blond-haired neighbour boy ride his BMX, for lying back on a couch and flipping the pages of a magazine. It wasn't a place to dream.

"Like old times." Avery threw the cars keys on the fridge. He twisted the top off a twixer of rye and chugged, held the bottle out to me.

I felt needy, and yet superior, in my ankle-length skirt, my patchouli oil perfume, my long hair parted down the middle and worn loose: a New Age woman living by morally elevated rules. I'd been reading Salman Rushdie, Toni Morrison, Italo Calvino. Writers my new friends had introduced me to. I knew that I'd left him, I'd squared up from the track, because of a compulsion to *matter*. Was I "making a difference" now?

I stopped myself from apologizing for not being "socially significant" enough, for the mess that surrounded him, for having left him when it was obvious he still needed my help.

He hugged me and said, "I always knew one day you'd leave me." We stood there in the kitchen doorway like that, hugging each other, for a long moment.

Later I told him about one of my co-workers at the Wilderness Committee, an Australian woman working her way around the world. "I really admire her," I said.

I told him I might travel with her.

I told him we'd talked about pooling our money to buy a sail-boat.

I told him that I wanted to travel, too, even if it meant travelling solo. That I had the address of an orphanage in Chiapas.

Hot Suffocation Hell

"I need to do this," I told my friends. I was twenty-five. I'd saved less money than my Australian co-worker but was more motivated to leave Vancouver as soon as I could. In the few months since Avery and I had been back in touch we'd been drinking together, smoking crack. I knew I was screwing up, that I had to leave town for my own good.

I romanticized the healing powers of movement, of what I'd learn eating breakfast anywhere, spending my day anywhere. Living simply, needing little, leaving no footprints. I'd backpack through the dust of Mexico, then Central America; I'd make it to Peru, ride on a *cayuca* down the Amazon, penniless and happy, relying on the generosity of river people to survive, surrounded by pet monkeys and brown slippery children. I'd hop on planes, pick up friends on rattling trains, address book swelling with numbers. The experience of lovers meeting once then never again would burn bright in my memory like a thousand tiny fires. Moving beyond selfishness. Rejoicing. Being free.

In December of 1996 I caught a one-way flight to Mexico City. From there I took a subway to the bus station and bought a cheap ticket to Oaxaca, planning to stop there for a few days' rest before heading to Chiapas. On Oaxaca's Pacific shore, in a town called Zipolite, Kyle waylaid me—his smile, his sea-green eyes, his hands as solid as the wooden table he placed them on.

He was an American anthropology major who spoke fluent Spanish and German. He was also bipolar and paranoid. Two years earlier he'd left his San Fernando halfway house and escaped across the U.S. border on a motorcycle. His charges stemmed from an armed carjacking that he described as a "misunderstanding."

One day, early on in our relationship, we sat on the beach and watched couples smoking weed as the sun set. Kids laughed in the turned-over cavities of fishing dories. Catholic schoolgirls pulled at boys' white shirts with hungry hands. There was an edge here in Zipolite. Cars trying not to run over the junkies passed out on the street. Drunks scaring tourists for cash. People with the crazed kind of eyes seen on born-again Christians, both full and empty.

Kyle invited me back to his cabana to smoke a joint. His beach house had a lime-treed courtyard furnished with gnarled, bleaching driftwood. The river stones placed among his exotic plants glowed like cairns marking a path on the moon. Ghost crabs skittered across his garden like alien invaders. He was only renting this home; he planned to build another on an arid slope by the *tortilleria*. He'd bought the land by saving his construction wages, putting it in a friend's name since foreigners couldn't own ocean property. I had yet to discover that he could memorize languages as easily as phone numbers and that he'd slept with every beautiful woman from here to Mexico City.

He talked about the expansive coral reef, the exquisite delicacy of purple sea fans, his love of the sea. Then we walked along the beach, our bare feet slapping the wet sand like paddles. It was easier to walk on the hard pack than on the shin-deep flour, but I was intensely aware of the sucking sound of each step—*shloop, shloop*—as incoming sheets of seawater tried to glue us in place. The moon looked silly, the *shloop* was silly. His arm around my shoulders swept a wide circle, keeping others back. I felt giddy in his embrace, swaddled and safe.

To get to Kyle's plot of land, *el terreno*, I had to take a *camioneta* to the post office then walk up a steep path to my left, following the smell of cook fires and the recorded sounds of Los Tigres del Norte. There Kyle would be, digging holes in the earth with a small shovel.

We'd been together a month, maybe two. I'd bring him support beams he'd prop up with an assortment of rocks. The frame measured six hundred square feet. Balanced unsteadily on the roof, he'd bark contradictory orders. Later we'd drink mezcal as fish cooked slowly over the coals.

Kyle—to love him or not. His full lips were always smiling, even when his eyes were worried or sad. His stomach was so lean that I could fit my fingers in the washboard spaces when he held his breath. It had frightened me at first, when we met, how hard he felt, like something not human, too perfect to be real.

He had an immense capacity for forgiveness; I could call him the vilest names and he'd carry on without a blink as if he hadn't heard.

I'd also seen Kyle rigid on the bed, catatonic, unable to speak for fourteen hours, muscles flexed to maximum capacity, eyes wide open like a doll's. He'd put his hand to his neck to find patterns in the beats of his pulse, an emotional tension within him making the exercise vital. People wanted him dead for secrets he knew: he said they'd planted spies in bookstores, cafés, taxis. He recorded his findings in a spiral-bound notebook, writing in code. His pseudo-research gave him a connection to a world larger than himself and a lifeline to place: for this I envied him.

I admired his ability to produce psychological fictions and his insatiable hunger for anything extraordinary. He was dying to be impressed.

And Kyle could give me what I wanted, even when my desire swung between two extremes: I wanted intimacy but needed detachment. His compulsive need for closeness, his fear of committing, and his manic depression helped forge a bond that felt familiar. I loved how, without believing in what I wished for, we could talk about going to Mexico City and then back to my home. "I think I can get used to being a Canadian," he said.

I wondered how long I'd find his vulnerability endearing. I'd gotten into the habit of ignoring his delusions about the Illuminati and about his teeth growing too big for his mouth. Six months into our relationship I began to flirt with other men, fantasizing that someone besides Kyle could be that magnet, first pulling and then repelling me.

Sometimes I dreamed, not about Kyle but about someone who looked exactly like him, holding in his arms a curly-headed toddler. Seen this way, Kyle resembled the capable, altruistic doctors I'd had met on the beach, young and handsome, on vacation with their European families.

Or I'd dream that he was calling my name. It would be morning, with few people on the road, the concrete bricks of the eastern wall yellow with sunlight, the air still cool, not yet water-thick. He'd be standing there dusty and alone at the gate, wearing his navy blue T-shirt with the white V-neck, holding his luggage, a bleached lock of hair hanging over one sunburned cheek. He'd have lost his red coral necklace. I'd hear his voice echoing as if from another dimension. Yet I'd feel no urgency to respond; I'd pretend it was a lullaby, letting the sound soothe me.

Even when he wasn't sick, paranoid, or hearing voices, I found myself thinking, Why me? We lived as opposites. He was wide awake when I went to sleep and still wide awake when I got up. He claimed he was guarding me. He held my head and put me to sleep with bedtime stories about poisonings. When he was manic I wouldn't wake up, preferring to curl into his rigid embrace and float away from coherent thought.

The severity of his bipolar disorder meant he lived on two planes at once. I thought my low self-esteem could be as danger-ous. He wouldn't let me leave *el terreno* because he wanted to protect me from demons. When I tried to go he said, "I can't let you leave. Don't you understand?" He looked at me as if I were a child. "It's for your safety."

We'd lasted this long—six months—because Kyle wanted a tradi-tional marriage and children and I knew that with him I'd never get either. His protective hands, his eyes wrapping me in their warm clutch the way a spider cocoons a ladybug, his confident voice insisting on all the things he could teach me. When we tum-bled into bed, breathless as wrestlers, it was compelling and passionate—because I never knew where I stood or whether he, or I, would be around the next day. He drew out of me that self-sacrifice essential to any worthwhile relationship, his needs drowning out the annoying buzz of my own. There was an element of desperation in our attachment, like the *shloop* of wet sand sucking at our feet.

Still, I could play at being the good wife even while breaking away from the role. Together we were the kind of couple that made people stare: good-looking, confident. His studied nonchalance, his exquisite symmetry, fulfilled my need for adventure. Our sex, as often as seven times a day, didn't involve true abandonment of oneself in another as much as constantly skirting the line between love and hate, making it so primal, so animal. Had we been animals we'd have already eaten each other. This consuming appetite, this desire, translated into something that felt, at least in the moment, more pure, more true than anything I'd had with anyone else, and kept me coming back for the easy way our bodies moved together like swimmer and river, our hair twining, hands clutching. I'd ignore his putdowns and affairs in exchange for what was immediate and simple and perfect, precisely because it could never be as complex as love. I felt absolute sacrifice and longing when he was inside me, longing even then, a longing that became only more profound over time.

Kyle and I made a living selling drugs in Zipolite, and, in the months since we'd partnered, we'd taken many trips together in claptrap buses to obscure parts of Mexico in search of new product, better deals. Every few weeks we bused the half day to Oaxaca, over the mountain road to Tehuacán, through Puebla to Teotitlán de Flores

Magón, Tuxtepec to Huautla de Jiménez, Kyle holding my head in his hands end route, muscles straining as I slept. He never let me drop as the bus bounced over potholes. In his embrace I began to swallow down sadness like the little girl I used to be, the one who played Barbies alone in the stairwell of the apartment project, scribbling their faces the colour of blood and leaving them to their wounds. The bus skirted black sands that sounded like sea spray against its sides. I tried not to think of my parents but, looking out the window, I did. We ate bananas and bruised tomatoes from roadside sellers who boarded at each stop. In this way we passed the time without ever saying a word.

In the cabin where we stayed, I asked the owner what his pet turtle ate and whether I could take it for a walk. When he refused, Kyle bought me a pair of silver turtle earrings as small and delicate as he made me feel.

Oaxaca City's nervous, polluted streets provided a mindless distraction from a coast filled with demons, from mountains thick with ghosts. The capital boasted more museums per capita than anywhere else in the state, and instead of the repetitive folk art the galleries featured photographic exhibitions of boys who dreamed of being television wrestlers. We went there for relief, like a vacation. One day Kyle refused to leave his hotel-room chair, insisting that the floor was covered in an invisible poison. Whenever I left the room to buy food I had to ask his permission, spell out my itinerary, my travel route, my expected time of return. Often I'd buy enough tuna and *charras* to last for days—I could never be sure he'd allow me to leave before we ran out of supplies.

Below us lived street musicians, and next door a young man who shared his room with his mother, who made and sold jewellery. There was a heroin dealer down the hall and vendors from out of town.

Frijol, the stray dog we'd lured home with a taco, sniffed for crumbs on our concrete floor. I sat on the tattered, knobbly bed-spread with half a beer in front of me while a radio blared from down the hall where our neighbours were high. Around me I set up a circle of objects that reminded me of myself—the twenty-dollar guitar I'd bought before leaving Vancouver, my journals, the sheet music I'd photocopied at the library back home intending to learn new songs while travelling. I looked at postcards from old friends and wrote a list of all the things I'd liked to do, trying to convince myself that the person I used to be still existed.

Outside the window slats night was falling on the courtyard. I could see the colonial buildings of the town square, the moun-tains in the background like a crumpled piece of paper tossed from heaven. In 1763 a Franciscan priest declared that, after creat-ing the world, God had put all the remaining mountains in Oaxaca.

"I'll be in the bathroom," I said.

Kyle held his breath as I crossed the room and closed the door.

The management had told us not to use the out-of-service toi-let across the hall but I'd used it anyway, not wanting to run the gauntlet of other rooms on the way to the working bathroom. Now, though, I passed it by and hurried toward the end of the hall. Through the small window at the end I could see the glowing lights of the liquor store.

Out on the street I looked longingly at the bottles locked away for the night behind the store's Closed sign. If I could have a drink, this might all seem funny: Kyle's voices, his visions, the stories he told—like the one about his mother when they were crossing the United States by car. He was six, maybe seven. The journey excited him: amusement parks and corn dogs, the carnival-like blending of one town into the next. They slept on the side of the highway.

Once he woke up in the middle of night. The doors were locked and he was alone.

"Why were you on the road?" I'd asked, as if the answer was important.

He thought for a moment. "I think we were looking for something."

"Maybe she went to buy milk," I said, "or smokes."

"She was a prostitute," he said. I'd told Kyle about my past, and since then prostitutes had come up more often in his stories. I'd given him the shorthand account, sketching in the when, why, and what, not mentioning Avery. I was still looking for answers to the deeper questions myself and hoped to defuse any potential argument over morals. I told him that "I was a teenage crack ho," which felt not only important but true. I even said it in a way to make it sound like the punch line of a joke, to imbue the experience with humour, deflate its gravity. If I'd hoped my confession would bring us closer, I was wrong. Kyle's symptomatic paranoia latched onto my past and spun delusions from its raw material. He saw rape where none existed, he saw my seduction of men I had no interest in.

Then, suddenly, his mother was also a prostitute. How do you know, I wanted to ask, but I knew this line of questioning would spiral into a deep pool of misunderstanding from which we'd never surface, as it always did. The two of us weren't an emotion but a habit, a symptom, as we moved toward a now-or-never.

Out on the street, in front of the liquor store, I flagged a cab. Asked the driver for a pen and paper. Wrote Kyle a note and told the driver to give it to the desk clerk. Then I sank into the sticky vinyl backseat and told him to go.

I couldn't stop crying. I told the driver that I'd left my lover.

"I have to disappear. Take me where I can blend and vanish into a crowd."

He nodded like a doctor. "*La zona turistica*. I see. You need to talk to your *paisanos*." He drove to the tourist district, where I vowed I'd drink a bottle of mezcal and talk to no one.

Before I got out of the cab I asked him, "Will it always be this way?"

"We make our lives happy or sad," the cab driver said. "But yes, it will always be this way. *Así es la vida*—such is life."

Squinting in the yellow-white light particular to this city, I watched families go into the Templo de la Compañía de Jesús. They strolled holding hands, bought candles and saint cards from the vendors outside, sharing a devotion I didn't have but craved: it wasn't that I didn't want to believe, it was that I'd forgotten how. I'd heard that in the chapel a statue of the Virgin of Guadalupe was adorned with prayers written in Spanish, English, Nahuatl, and four dialects of Zapotec. Instead of praying, I smoked.

Children charmed their parents into buying them helium balloons shaped like cartoon characters, cotton candy, small cheap toys not meant to last more than a week. I loved to see children so well behaved, the obvious pride of their mothers and fathers. And I loved to see the men, with their big-chested embraces and a macho but attractive sense of ownership, bestowing a level of care upon the women. These women knew how to be ladies; these men knew how to protect what was theirs.

The night grew cold. Sitting in the centre of the square, I tried to forget what it felt like to have a pair of arms around me to ward off the chill.

I listened to a marimba band. Children selling chicle and toy birds saw my face and stayed away; so did the women with grilled corn, the men with crutches. Even the blind accordion player felt my confusion and did not hold out his hand.

Kyle found me in the square. He'd been looking all over town, wearing his board shorts and a heavy parka.

He said: "I love you more than I've ever loved anything."

He said: "You needed something to love that much and I'm it."

He said: "I want to be together in fifty years."

He said: "We'll get married in June."

I lowered my head, raised my eyebrows. "Who says?"

"What if you got pregnant? Think about that." He clutched my wrist till it hurt.

Months later, back in Canada, alone, I would recall the heat of our last day on the land. I was helping Kyle build the roof. He'd curtained one side of the *ramada* with a layer of palm fronds and wanted me to hang my hammock inside. I refused. It was an unstable structure and I knew better than to trust myself to something so unbalanced.

I'd passed Kyle palm fronds knowing they'd never keep the rain off the floor. I knew one strong wind would send the fronds crashing on our heads. Knew this house would never be completed, would never be real.

I had returned from Mexico with no place to stay, no job, and five hundred dollars in my pocket. I'd let myself down by not volunteering at the orphanage, and I hid my shame from friends who asked, "How was the trip?"

"Yeah, good," I'd say, a make an inane comment about tacos.

The nude beach. Partying my ass off. I didn't tell them I'd been irrelevant, insignificant—even detrimental, a loose spore hitching a ride on the wind, trying to make roots where I didn't belong.

I'd wanted to grow, fungi-like, into respectability. I'd proven to myself I was a failure.

The few pots and pans I'd collected from a thrift store after leaving Avery awaited me in a downtown storage locker along with my clothes, but I had no place to put them. Then I met Phillip, a close friend of the Australian woman I'd almost travelled with, but who had decided to linger in Canada longer than I wished to stay. He asked if I needed a place to crash.

Phillip was an artist. He and his roommate lived in an illegal warehouse space in Vancouver's Downtown Eastside, blocks from two dozen skid-row pubs. The soles of his combat boots were attached with duct tape. He cultivated the adolescent "I'm gonna shock you" affectation, trying to prove to me and everyone else that darkness streaked his psyche, his vulnerable qualities peeking through the facade. I could see him attracting the type of woman who enjoyed saving lost puppies and Mason jars to can homemade soup.

But still. As we sat drinking two-dollar pints of beer in a bar full of cockroaches, I could see the life I wanted to be inside of, the life I wanted inside of me. He had an art degree and a group of friends who used words like "contrapuntal" and "deconstructionism" in casual conversation. He offered me entry into a world where to write was a calling and not a hobby, where I too could learn to speak in -isms and -ologies at potlucks over plates of tabbouleh.

We walked to his studio, meandering through broken bottles of rice wine, windshield glass glinting on the sidewalk next to cars with no stereos, condom wrappers blowing like petals. The studio space had been a bowling alley, a stash for bootlegged whisky, an opium den. I noticed that it occupied the same block as the Golden Crown trick hotel where I used to take dates I didn't trust, but I said nothing. The space extended under the sidewalk where purple squares of glass inlaid into the concrete glowed eerily, illuminating our faces.

We descended a flight of stairs. Canvases leaned against walls, pressed demurely or mysteriously behind furniture salvaged from the alley: a dented filing cabinet, a plastic Coppertone display table dripping with jars of turpentine and tubes of acrylic paint.

I stood with my feet shoulder-width apart in front of the breast-high oscillating fan. It was tarnished, dusty on the base, and kept sticking with a click at the end of each arc.

Phillip painted as he talked.

"I went to art school," he said, his back to me, "not 'cause I thought it was the right thing do but because it couldn't possibly be the wrong thing. Then I got a job as a line cook." He moved from one canvas to the next, canvases that were lined up side by side like paper dolls, their elbows touching, painting a line or a stroke on each. "The only thing that set me apart from the rest of the guys was my art. The guys that worked there were so ordinary and sad. There were guys in their fifties who'd been there since they were fifteen. The money was good, but I swore I'd never end up like them."

"Isn't that a bit harsh?"

"It is if they were happy, but who could be? Anyhow, I made sure everyone knew I'd be quitting once I'd saved enough money to rent a studio and just paint. That way I wouldn't have to social-ize with them. All the guys stopped asking me to go to the pub with them after work."

I kicked off my boots. My feet made damp prints on the concrete floor as I walked around avoiding the spots covered with oil paint.

Phillip put his palette down on the dented filing cabinet and then turned the paintings to the wall, one by one, and faced me, covered in streaks of titanium white and cadmium yellow.

We lay down on the sheetless futon on the paint-splashed floor. He smelled like a boy, unwashed, the city in his clothes. I liked that his smell didn't come from a bottle of cologne, that what you saw was what you got. The studio had no interior walls. Phillip and I listened for the sound of his roommate's footsteps in the stairwell, his key in the door, but the footsteps never came. We had sex. It was very casual. Afterward he ran his hand over my body with the wonder of a boy and the eye of a formally trained artist.

We dressed and bought a can of beans from the twenty-four-hour Lucky Mart with the ninety-two cents Phillip had managed to scrounge. We ate the half loaf of white bread he had in the fridge—which he locked to keep out the rats, mice, cockroaches. Beans and bread. We ate with our fingers, listening to the footsteps above us. Hookers' stilettos tapping like a bedtime staccato. Dealers' sneakers running from police, the odd rattle of dented shopping-cart wheels.

Though chiefly a painter, Phillip did installation work, too, and was represented by Third Avenue Gallery, which hosted openings once a month. To these functions Phillip always wore a bowling shirt with a pair of Dickies work pants. The pants were both trendy and functional—like him. Big ox-blood boots were his only footwear. Of course, he had flip-flops for the summer, $1.99 Chinatown specials.

I grilled him on the logistics of living without really earning a living. His ability to romanticize his poverty verged on irritating, since of course for him it was a choice. As we lay in bed, listening to water dripping from his ceiling, Phillip told me he wished he could move to a different studio in a cleaner part of the city. He hadn't had an art show in six months, he said; hadn't sold any paintings in eight. He thought of himself as a painter, but I knew that sometimes his parents paid the bills. He pointed to the black mould that had begun to grow from the ceiling, stalactites in an urban concrete cave, and the water that had already ruined the throw rug. He collected the drips in rusty pots and dumped them in the toilet down the hall. "How's that for you?" he said.

"If it's money, you could get a part-time job," I said, the mould reaching down like wagging fingers, as if scolding Phillip for complaining about living under the Argyle Hotel where people plugged up the plumbing by flushing their needles.

"There's some people who can do both. I can't," he said.

"So where do you go? If they kick you out?"

"You have to ask yourself what matters in the big picture," he said, throwing his hands above his head. "How many people know what it's like to be this close to homeless? Too many people call themselves artists who won't sacrifice a thing for it. They've got their cushy jobs, their cushy lives. For me, *this* is life."

He appalled me and impressed me. To have a university education and live like this? He exercised a brand of elegant bohemianism that gave him licence to be above it all.

Phillip's roommate drove a taxi and supported a woman with two small children who weren't his. He used to drink until his esophagus burst, almost killing him. Now he battled a weakness for soft drinks and a missionary complex.

He lit a cigarette as I leaned against the brick of the alley wall where sunlight glinted off the wings of hundreds of flies hovering above the dumpsters.

"I gave Phillip the money," I told him.

"What money?"

"My share of the rent." I'd landed a nude-modelling job. It paid fifty dollars an hour, even if clients were neither regular nor steady. "I don't want you to think I'm abusing your hospitality."

He cleared his throat, shook his head. "Our boy."

"You didn't get it? I gave him cash," I said.

He tossed his greying ponytail, turning his head toward the street and exhaling the smoke away from my face. "I'll bet you did."

To flesh out the modelling I started busking on the corner of Water and Cambie streets. From the studio I'd walk the two blocks to Gastown, where tourists with little white socks and cameras slung around their necks strolled on cobblestone streets, photographing landmarks like the steam clock and the Gassy Jack statue, and paid the equivalent of half our month's rent to eat in restaurants with "fusion" in their name. I stationed myself in front of a shop that sold carved totem poles and leather goods and began to play the guitar I'd picked up in Mexico. The first one had broken, its strings snapping like my plans to volunteer, the high E ricocheting like a bullet to slice open my arm. I'd gotten butterfly stitches in the office of a doctor who listened to Mozart while disinfecting my wound. I couldn't play; I'd learned ukulele in elementary school and taught myself what I knew now: six songs, on an endless loop.

On days when people flung pennies into my guitar case, or asked me to make change, I came home dejected. I'd been trying to publish my work, and ever since moving in with Phillip I'd been sending off stories about my travels in Oaxaca. Some days I couldn't even afford the postage for submissions to literary magazines.

I never paid for items I could get for free. I picked a sweater out of the garbage in the bathroom of a nearby drop-in centre where I took my hot showers. I knew what time of day to find the biggest cigarette butts outside the Sinclair Centre office tower, fresh, half-smoked specimens. On a special day I bought cheap Drum tobacco, but I had to be careful with it because people on the street (like me) liked to bum smokes and would take my pouch and roll a cigarette thicker than my thumb if I let them. Once a week I'd buy a single tailor-made cigarette from a convenience store on Hastings Street, the same one that sold individual tea bags for a nickel.

I met the scrap-metal collectors with their shopping carts, the guy who sold stolen cheese from Safeway, the guy who offered me a sip of his Aqua Velva. I met a man who found people parking spots for a couple of bucks. If that didn't pan out he invented poems, on the spot, for any amount of spare change. His name was Sean and he liked that I was a writer. He was the son of a diplomat, had been raised in Latin America, and could sell drugs in Spanish. He was the kind of guy who worked every angle, even when he was drunk or high. Sean hustled, he sold stolen rollerblades, and—unlike the alcoholics and the dumpster divers, the people who walked to the twenty-four-hour convenience store to buy a weevil-ridden package of instant noodles in their pyjamas, who stepped like zombies into the street without looking right or left, impervious to ambulance sirens—he wasn't down here because life had happened to him. Neither was I. We watched a man eating ice cream with his fingers out of a pail he'd salvaged from a dumpster and a woman hawking, for thirty-five cents, a tailor-made smoke with lipstick on the filter. No, we weren't like them.

I was proud of myself one day after having earned sixty dollars, twenty of them American, given to me by a rich guy from Miami for singing a song in Spanish. I'd been bragging about it, improving the story with each telling. Saying how the Downtown Eastside had taken me on as a sort of apprentice.

I'd been up to the library already, stolen the toilet paper we needed. When it began to rain tourists scrambled into shops and locals found dry spaces in which to shelter. I stared at the falling drops. Sean, his cigarette burning in his hand, watched them too. Even the clerk from the tourist store behind us left the register to stand in the doorway and look out. It was as if the cloth sheets draping the world had slipped to crash around our feet, collecting and pooling. The drops played and tumbled and splashed on my boots where they shone; the world was, for now, clean and simple. Soon the streets were flowing. The rain landed on my fingers, calloused from playing songs I didn't know all the words to.

Phillip was working on a portrait. A commission. In exchange for an oil painting of his daughter, the landlord would knock off our back rent. He was a good landlord who appreciated that we weren't junkies or running an after-hours, and who fancied himself a patron of the arts. Phillip had started blocking in her image, a young woman posing before a fireplace, but had then painted over the entire canvas. I lost count of how many times he did this before turning the painting to the wall, where it had had been facing for days.

——

I wrote as if in competition with Phillip. I finished what I was calling a novel; then, inexplicably, I took it and cut it into pieces, spreading them out from one corner of our vast warehouse studio to the other. As if I could repair my fractures, I taped them back together again in another order. Then another. Nothing satisfied me. I threw sections away. Penned new sections. Forced Phillip to live encircled by slices of paper that lifted from the floor and floated in mid-air every time the heavy door to the studio opened or closed. I thought I was trying to prove that I was as good an artist as Phillip. Yet the more I worked on this "novel," the more I found myself thinking about the past.

I wrote: "The Yellow Cab rolled past the house with a pavement square for a front yard and stopped in front of the one with the bug-eaten morning glory vines, the one where a Rottweiler was pushing his nose through the living room blinds." The new material was old material filtered through the person I was trying to become.

The next day it dawned on me. To be whole, I needed to integrate whoever I'd been, even Michelle, into who I was now.

Maybe the answer lay with Avery.

In reality, I was rationalising the draw my old life still had, the good a part of the bad, impossible to separate.

I began to see him a few times a week. He was running another grow op now and suggested I trim his crop for twenty-five dollars an hour.

"Honk your horn," I told the cab driver when we arrived. He eyed me in the rear-view mirror. Two blasts. *Wah-wah*, like an injured goose.

Avery cracked the door open and peered outside. Even from this distance I could see that his face was bathed in sweat. I motioned to him. He shoved the door closed and a few seconds later pulled it back open, kneeing the dog in the chest to keep her down. He had on a tie-dyed undershirt and red nylon shorts, a plastic shower cap, opaque from grease, hiding his long hair.

Avery came to the driver's-side window in his bare feet. His jaw was tight and he was grinding his teeth. "How much?" he said, having trouble speaking. This always happened when he got high.

"Twenty-two fifty."

Avery lowered his head to read the meter. I opened the door of the cab and stepped into garish sunshine, waiting while Avery handed the driver the fifty-dollar bill folded up in his hand. He collected the change in his open palm, even the coins. I wondered about that—whether he was broke, and how broke that might be—but didn't say anything. I followed him up the stairs as the cab drove away.

"Be a heat score, then, will you?" Avery said, opening the door. "What did you do that for?"

He meant the horn. "Sorry," I said. "Take a pill. I won't do it again."

He stared at me, weighing whether to curse me out, as if I'd gotten his neighbours' attention to do whatever his paranoid mind had conjured up.

I ignored him and closed the door behind us as his new dog, a white pit bull not yet two years old, rushed about our feet. I reached for his pack of Du Mauriers on the kitchen counter and rummaged under restaurant flyers for a book of matches.

"Get!" Avery said to the dog. He pointed with his finger. "Go lie down." She slicked her ears back, tucked her tail between her legs, and, never taking her eyes off Avery, slunk through the doorway to the living room, where she lay down next to the couch.

I began opening drawers. "Aren't there any matches around here?"

"Basement." He headed for the door leading to the unfinished space where the plants grew. "You coming?"

The stairs were steep, uncarpeted plywood. They creaked with each footstep.

"I might be driving," Avery said, palming the wall as though it was holding him up.

"What's that?"

"Next week. A load to Edmonton. Five G's."

"Cool . . . That'd be good, eh?"

A bare bulb illuminated three kitchen chairs placed in a triangle around a pile of untrimmed bud on newspaper, the edges of the room in shadow. The smell of pot, from the pile on the floor and from the plants that grew on the other side of the flimsy divider, was overpowering.

I picked up a branch and a pair of scissors. "So, you broke? You got money to pay me?"

More pot was laid out to dry on large window screens raised up on bricks.

"I'll have your money soon," he said.

I picked up another willowy branch with smaller branches that shot off in all directions. I waved it, examining buds no bigger than my thumb. It was a shit crop.

Avery held small silver scissors from a store in Chinatown up to the light. He put them down. "I'm going to have a hit." He bent over a candle I hadn't noticed, hidden by the pile of bud closest to him. Above the divider he'd scrawled *Pimp Daddy* in black magic marker on an exposed two-by-four. Avery had hidden his crack pipe, a glass straight shooter, in the wall frame where *Avery + Darcy* was written. His new girlfriend. Holding his straight shooter in one hand, he ripped two matches from the cardboard pack with the other, then leaned over the tea light and held their sulphur heads over the flame until they flared. My palms began to sweat at the sound, the sizzle, the sweet smell.

He took a hit and passed me the pipe, still smoking; I pursed my lips and sucked while he lit new matches for me. Like an old married couple, we predicted and then completed each other's movements. He raised the matches to reheat the remaining shard of crack as I lifted my head to the pipe and began inhaling, nectar swirling into my lungs.

"Slower, slower," he said.

I'd heard of escaped convicts sucking air through bamboo straws to remain hidden beneath the black, stinking, brackish water of swamps. I sucked more slowly, the way they must have, drawing enough air to live, not enough to be noticed.

"That's it. Keep going." When the matches burned out he threw them to the floor; I nodded and he lit two more. My shoulders lifted with the effort of sucking. Even in my seat I felt like I was standing on my tiptoes. When my lungs were full I pulled the pipe from my mouth, dead, no smoke, crack gone. Good hit. Nothing left in the pipe. I held my breath for as long as I could, and when my lungs verged on exploding I curled my finger toward him, a smile spreading on my lips. He lowered his head and placed his lips on mine. In a large rush, dizzy, I exhaled the smoke into his mouth. Then I sat back in my chair, my ears ringing, dazed. When Avery exhaled fifteen seconds later the smoke streaming from his mouth was strong enough to reach across the room.

"That was a good one," he said.

"Yeah, holy, that was a good one."

For the next hour and a half we alternated between the basement and the living room, going upstairs to listen to music, going downstairs when we needed another hit, match flame honeying down the crack on a bed of ash, scorched spoons on the coffee table, thin columns of smoke.

Mountain of Knives

The inventory of my life so far included one poem in a Belgian literary magazine, a handful of newspaper articles, no toaster, no winter coat, no money. I'd written a travel piece about Belize, an op-ed piece about discrimination against interracial couples, and a personal essay about losing my Christian faith. The *Vancouver Sun* newspaper had an arts editor who liked my work. For every four articles painstakingly typed on Phillip's manual machine, he took one. And paid me.

I was high but coming down, which may have accounted for why I was marching in exasperation across the intersection toward home, wanting to get to the studio and shut the door behind me as fast as I could. Everyone looked crazy. I wondered if those pushing shopping carts teetering with Franciscan Sisters blankets and sick dogs and recyclable bottles and slabs of greasy cardboard had lost part of their mind on purpose, to justify the search, or in all their muttering insanity their minds had snapped. I wasn't one of them. I tried to walk with a sense of pride, keeping my things-on-the-go self-image, past the emaciated hookers who worked outside our front door, dealers dealing, junkies shooting up with puddle water, ambulances reviving overdoses. From the outside I looked like anyone with a habit. But I was a writer, living with an artist. What did people know about that?

I'd had a few pregnancy scares in Zipolite, when my period came late or not at all. On my return to Canada, not having had a period in three months, I felt sure Kyle's baby was growing inside me. Before I got the chance to take a test my period came fast and hard, making me wonder: Was this a miscarriage?

I visited my parents on the heels of this "loss." My German grandmother as well as an aunt and uncle had chosen to visit my mother during their vacation that year. Prompted by their arrival, I caught a ferry boat over. Out in the sunshine on my parents' deck, surrounded by potted flowers buzzing with bees, I said to my mother, "Well, I'm twenty-six years old. That means I have a couple good years left to get pregnant, right? I want kids. Within the next year or two, I'll find someone." I envisioned meeting my life partner. "After that, my chances of having a Down's baby go way up, don't they?"

Afraid of hurting my feelings, my mother refrained from pointing out my astounding naïveté, the impulsivity of my plan.

Within what I thought of as my perfect time frame, I became pregnant in the fall of that year.

My doctor confirmed the results. Then he hesitated, looking down at his clipboard. "Is this a happy occasion?"

I said yes.

"Well, in that case, mazel tov."

In the studio, cross-legged on the futon and surrounded by the detritus of our creative endeavours, I gave Phillip the news. Then I said that not keeping it would be tantamount to asking myself in the years to come, "Which one of our babies did we kill?"

I used the words "our" and "we" when I meant "mine" and "I."

I wanted to be a mother. Phillip's lack of any memorable response seemed agreement enough.

My driving motivation could be distilled thusly: "The writer must learn to neither evade nor waste any personal experience."

It was a quote I'd read and misunderstood as one should selfishly pursue all life had to offer—and now, specifically, that I should have a child. I'd be able to write from a richer self, from the perspective of a mother. The only way to do that properly was to give birth. Only the real thing could satisfy true writerly curiosity.

I gave no thought to whether my life would change, my decision on par with buying a new pair of shoes that I could tuck away in the closet at will.

In other words, having a child was simply adding to my life.

When I told the welfare office they increased my stipend so that I could afford the necessary vitamins and supplements. I quit drinking, continued smoking, and I kept on busking, wondering often what the tiny baby in my gut thought of my music. Was it comforting? Or did it tumble and toss them in their amniotic bath?

I was improving my art. No way would I become like so many other women who'd tell their children, "I used to be a writer." Painter, dancer, photographer, brain surgeon. "Then you came along and I had to give it all up."

Patti, my writer friend, had suffered at the hands of such a mother.

Instead I'd become the kind of mother my Australian co-worker had had. She'd been raised on the road in third-world countries, following a mother who bought trinkets to flip for a profit, until the endless shifting of towns became home, movement as home.

I visited the doctor regularly.

I wasn't gaining much weight, but I was five foot two, half Vietnamese. Of course my baby would be small.

One evening a friend named Junko and her husband asked Phillip and me when we were going to have a baby.

"Well, actually," Phillip said, "in August."

"August?"

Their joy and excitement embarrassed me.

"Are you ready?" they asked. Ready for the imminent, lasting turn in my life. And yet I still believed parenthood meant that only the writing would change.

My foolishness staggers me. Had I learned nothing about responsibility back when I volunteered at the hospital for handicapped children? If I had an inkling of what parenthood entailed, I'd blocked it out.

All that mattered now was that I was the smartest writer, the smartest artist on earth, for recognizing and capitalizing on such a rich muse. If someone had asked whether I'd like to be in the middle of the ocean surrounded by sharks I'd have said yes, to have the experience to draw on. Cultivate the most unusual experiences you can because what surrounds you shapes you, and what shapes you shapes your words. How else to deepen your voice, your scope?

On the other hand, had I not been so naive, I wouldn't have the two children I have today. Fast-forward five years to my second pregnancy. By now I knew that motherhood was work, but was still naive enough to believe Phillip when he said this second baby was all about him. "One child to replace each of us," he said, talking about posterity. "All you have to do is give birth. Then hand the baby over, I'll do everything."

Rewind. Phillip's mother, Christine, ran a three-room B&B on Mayne Island, one of the Gulf Islands situated between Vancouver Island to the west and mainland British Columbia to the east. Mayne Island was a verdant paradise populated by wealthy weekenders, aging hippies, loggers, crab fishermen, and young families. During the week Phillip's father worked on the mainland, living in a small apartment with his mother in White Rock.

When we arrived on the island at Christmastime, the swelling around Christine's eyes, her belly stretching her waistband, worried me. She didn't look as though she was dying, but her eyes and mouth and nose had rearranged themselves in a way that couldn't be attributed to weariness or frustration. She stuffed the Christmas turkey and stirred the gravy, her eyes bulging, her hands as puffy as balloons.

I wasn't yet used to this family, their silences, their ability to ignore impending doom with a stiff upper lip and another pint, so I wasn't about to shriek "Why haven't you seen a doctor?" I did ask Christine if she was in pain. She said it didn't hurt, that "I just look like I'm pregnant." She forced a laugh.

We hadn't told her *I* was pregnant. Not yet. I'd only known for a few days myself. At the doctor's office he'd paused before asking me to fill out a questionnaire that asked how much I smoked, how often I drank, how many alcoholic beverages before I felt drunk? Once he'd reviewed my answers he added me to the high-risk mothers list, meaning I'd have the pleasure of delivering in British Columbia's best facility, the Women's Hospital. At the time, I thought I owed the privilege to being short-statured.

With Christmas over, Christine reluctantly agreed to see a doctor. ("Stop making such a fuss.") She'd asked us to look after the house and so I set to work, sweeping and scrubbing away the holiday grime. I wanted her to like me. Meanwhile, Phillip's father drove her to the mainland, calling later that day to let us know she'd been booked into Surrey Memorial for tests.

Two days later she was dead. Gone. Kidney failure. Her puffy appearance had been a final symptom of a progressive disease.

That night we drove back from the hospital, passing late-hanging Christmas lights along the way. At one point, as the traffic light turned green, I looked over at Phillip and asked him how he was doing. "Oh, I'm good," he said, as if I'd offered him a drink or another slice of pie. The stiff upper lip, the British stoicism—he wasn't fine. How could he be? Red, stop. Green, go. Death, Life. All I could think about was that Christine would never meet her grandchild.

After the funeral we returned to Mayne. As Phillip and I cleaned and packed and sorted, I pushed away tears, ruminating on how unfair it was that this woman's life, a person I'd barely known, should fit so neatly into cardboard boxes, the way mine had once fit into a backpack. How small anyone's life really was.

———

A couple of friends who'd heard what we were planning looked at us incredulously over pints of beer. We were seated at the Ivanhoe, a skid-row bar I'd often used as a test when meeting someone new: if they agreed to venture into the melee of skaters, skinheads, crusty punks, factory shift workers, and men who rode around on stolen bicycles selling stuffed animal key chains from their basket, we might become friends. If they said "Hell, no," the friendship was over before it had begun.

After Christine's death I'd dyed my hair the colour of a rotting eggplant. My logic ran like this: having purple hair could mean I'd lose customers at the nude modelling agency. To defy the manager's warning was to seize the day, but to refuse cash from amateur porn photographers was to defy death. Life was too short to spend any time doing what you didn't want to do.

"*You're* planning to run a B&B?"

"What's so crazy about that?"

They looked at my purple hair. Phillip's shaved head.

"He's got his Food Safe," I said, meaning his certification to serve food.

They continued staring. Both were skinheads, one of whom worked the door at Ivanhoe and didn't mind it when he had to throw Gulf Island rainbow-dreadlocked hippies out onto the street.

"I've worked as a line cook," Phillip added.

They drank deeply from their pint mugs as if to say "Good luck with that, we'll see you back here in a month."

We skipped town, still owing back rent. We loaded our books and Phillip's paints and canvases into his roommate's truck; the rest I put in boxes marked "Free" and set out on the curb. That included my working clothes from the track, the ones I'd turned my back on but had stopped short of giving away: miniskirts and tank tops, high-waisted shorts, short-waisted jackets. I watched as women perused five- and six-inch stilettos and scooped up the clothes I'd earned a fortune in.

Working at the Wilderness Committee meant that I'd been so broke I'd come close to returning to the track. Getting rid of the clothes, like dyeing my hair, was closing a door. If any good were to come of Christine's death, it was through the life Phillip and I would make for ourselves in the place she'd called home.

If our friends had wondered whether we could run a B&B, our guests must have wondered the same thing, because when I'd open the door with my purple hair a few nearly took off running. I did most of the food prep and most of the cleaning. Phillip cooked on the frontlines, and we both answered the phone to take bookings.

The rich, stale house. So many rooms, gleaming with polish. Brass candlesticks, ceramic vases, floral prints. Cherubs painted on the walls. Thirty-foot vaulted ceilings in the living room, as impressive as they were impractical. Masses of brilliant overhead space made the house hard to heat; I was always cold. I thought about the original Mayne Island inhabitants, the Tsartlip, who'd been fishing the Salish Sea for three thousand years. I thought of the farmers, loggers, rum-runners who came after, who built homes with the spirit of adventurers, explorers, and travellers, and who certainly awoke with the sunrise. Once again I was a modern-day adventurer, as I'd been on the streets, or so I fancied myself. I was happy to have stability and wanted to honour Christine's memory—my unborn child's grandmother's memory—by putting all I had into this venture. At the same time, it was hard not to feel guilty about how we'd landed the place, about hitching a free ride.

Through the arched windows I could see the mouth of the bay, the road into town. Skinny, half-naked alders lined the road, along with maples and honeysuckle. Life could be as simple as making a home, having a child, enjoying the view.

I loved the beach at night. I never used a flashlight to find my way. What was the worst that could happen? I watched ants zigzag across the bone-white, moonlike surface, logs laced with the filigree of termites, the stain of seagull shit. The buzz of a boat motor rising in the cool while Phillip worked at home, paintbrush in hand. Starlight glanced off a sailboat bobbing offshore in the low tide of seaweed stew. The sand scratched my shoulders. I wiped my chin with the back of my hand and stood stiffly. I began the walk back, closed my eyes and reopened them, convincing myself I could see in the dark.

The porch light was off. Phillip was sitting in the darkness on the bench seat we'd removed from an old truck and used as a couch, smoking a joint. He tapped the edge of it against an empty cat food tin so persistently that no trace of ash remained.

"Pleasant outing?" he asked.

"I guess."

I pulled the Adirondack chair across the deck and sat next to him. Phillip in his Chinatown flip-flops, his T-shirt with the image of a half-naked 1950s pin up screen printed on the front, checked cut-offs. Slender as a lizard, his legs stretched out in front of him and crossed at the ankles, his toes so long they looked more like fingers.

"Chilly tonight," I said. I looked up at the stars, then took his hand and placed it on my stomach. "Feel that?" I said. "I've been thinking about how it's going to be when the baby's born."

He pressed his fingers into my flesh and smiled strangely. Then he pulled his hand away.

"Do you want to see a doctor?" He crushed his joint out in the empty tin.

"I haven't missed a single appointment."

"I know about your legs."

"What?" I said.

"I was watching a program on TV two nights ago. There's a woman in Alberta who's just been labelled a dangerous offender, you may have heard of her," Phillip said. "She slashes herself, too."

I did not take my eyes off the stars. From the bottom you had nowhere to look but up.

"Why?" he said.

"Leave me alone."

He examined the backs of his fingers, which he did whenever he felt conflicted. "I believe you need help."

"I can't go to a doctor."

"Why can't you?"

"Because."

"Because why?"

"I said I can't talk about it *now*."

"That woman in Alberta, she—"

"Look, another star," I said.

"How bad are they? Do you need stitches?"

"It doesn't have anything to do with you."

"How am I supposed to react to this?"

"Don't be mad. Jesus." I became terrified. "Listen, I did crazy things. Like, as a kid. Sticking sewing needles into my fingers and walking around. Everyone did. Or I'd go a full day just eating an apple. It's nothing."

"It's not funny," Phillip said. "Don't make it funny. It's sick."

"Yeah, well."

"Is life with me that bad? Is that what you're trying to say? What did I do?"

"Nothing. You never did anything."

I burst into tears and escaped into the house. I locked myself into the en suite, though there was no need; he wasn't following.

I sat on the pink bath mat, leaning against the shower stall, my heart knocking. My dirty secret was out. I'd been cutting myself since Mexico. The need came and went like a tooth abscess, festering out of sight until some irritation brought the pain to the surface.

I hid the marks on my body even from myself, refusing to look at them in the shower. I didn't know how to stop and I needed help. I hated that I'd never be able to stop alone. I hated knowing that I relied on men. That my life, like Picasso's art, could be divided into periods: the Blue Period, the Johnny Period, the Will Period, the Jay, Avery, Phillip Periods. I felt tossed to fate like those tiny stones the waves threw back on shore. From a distance, beyond the kelp soup and ropes of seaweed, no one, not even me, could tell if they were coming or going. My whole problem was looking for help outside myself for what I needed most.

I felt like a moving picture projected on the wall. Of course it was wrong to feel that I existed only when a man wanted me. To cut myself to feel more alive. It was wrong and I, like all guilty creatures, had to look away from the distortion.

Celestial Empire

My rambunctious child is running roughshod over the B&B's enforced sterility, where disinfection and silence are the rules of the house.

I'd walked out of the hospital with Jet swaddled and crying under my arm, wondering when I'd be caught like a thief and stopped with a baby I had no idea what to do with. I learned how to bake my own bread, how to stretch forty dollars over two weeks. Money was scarce—the B&B hardly paid for itself. We gave the money to Phillip's father, who used it to pay the accountant, and at the end of the day nothing remained. We ate the guests' breakfast leftovers after they checked out. I cleaned houses on the side and often took Jet to work with me, so great was Phillip's reluctance to mind her—he needed time to paint. Domesticity was smothering him, he said. Unless I had laundry to do, his basement studio was off-limits.

Every Wednesday morning I'd get into my rusty Ford truck and drive to a local mother's living room where pudgy-fingered kids ate dirt and mashed bananas into their hair. This was Mayne Island's "playgroup."

One of the moms had set up a slip-and-slide with a black tarp and dish soap. The toddlers frolicked in the yard, rolled in the bubbles, squirted each other with a green garden hose. Pink Popsicle sticks littered the wooden porch, as did we, basking in the July warmth. A car drove by and I could sense the male driver looking at us, six or seven women, breastfeeding, with stretch-marked bellies pressed up to the sun, eyes closed like lizards. My face grew scarlet. Nothing about my appearance distinguished me, yet it felt crucial that this man, this perfect stranger, should be able to tell me apart, to know that I'd never be like *these mothers* in their pastel cotton smocks, discussing the links between autism and vaccines and recipes for homemade play dough. How had I ended up in a group that consisted of stay-at-home moms anyway? As if the role of motherhood supplied a unifying bond?

I was lonely. I missed the city. All I wanted to do was run. Toss off my load and run, long and hard and fast.

The streets had taught me many things, but not how to move forward as a whole person while keeping my past a secret.

I rearranged furniture and drank to shut my eyes. Who was I if I couldn't even look at a sunset without pain? I carried on writing, a maladaptation to modify anger and sadness, regurgitating it in bursts like a bad meal until I felt empty

I needed to go back to school. Improve myself, thus improve my outlook. Meeting Phillip, I'd wanted to soak away my past in an intellectual soup, surround myself with conversations about Glenn

Gould, Marcel Duchamp, Jean-Paul Sartre, Carl Jung, Heidegger.
I needed to reclaim that desire and run with it.

My second child, Maisie, was born in 2004 when I was thirty-two,
in the spring of the year I returned to school.

I was still cleaning houses. As I scrubbed a toilet or polished a
shower stall, I'd consider the only two paths I saw before me: student loans or saving enough to get my degree piecemeal.

The atmosphere at home had grown toxic. Phillip blamed me
for his inability to paint, said his creative block and his lack of
recognition were the result of having a family. He'd fly into a rage
if Jet spilled their soup, punch a hole through the wooden slats of
the closet door.

I'd applied to the University of Victoria, and thanks to a slim
portfolio of published work, had been given an advanced place-
ment in its creative writing program.

Leaning toward student loans, with an eye to eventually moving to Victoria, I scouted daycares online. I found one that accepted
children younger than three at a facility near the university, by a
forest called Haro Woods with a view of the ocean.

In that way the universe has, the daycare was on the grounds of
the hospital for handicapped children where I'd volunteered twenty
years earlier. Where I'd sat in the lap of a man later convicted of
child abuse. If it was a sign, I didn't know of what.

I made the drive to the Village Bay ferry terminal on Mayne
Island, tried to entertain Jet on the two-and-a-half-hour boat ride
with a half bag of Cheerios and two crayons, breastfed Maisie,
drove past billboards on the highway from Swartz Bay to Victoria
with both children screaming in their car seats, picked up the

government subsidy application form in a cramped, windowless office, and then did the whole thing in reverse. When I returned to Victoria a week later—drive, ferry, drive—the woman behind the counter at the government office looked at me, scratching her ear with a pencil before saying a word. "It says you're married."

"Yes, common-law."

"It says your husband is unemployed."

"Um, yes. Well, I mean, he's a painter. But he doesn't have, like, you know, a real job. With a paycheque. I need this subsidy to go back to school."

She told me that, owing to Phillip's unemployment, she couldn't approve my request. "Since he's at home? So he can look after her."

I thought of Ann Landers's advice when it came to relationships. Are you better off with him or without him? Now, I had to admit, the answer was without.

The woman must have seen me holding back tears. She leaned forward, her gaze softening. "Does he have any issues with drugs or alcohol?" she asked gently. "Any mental health problems?"

I thought of how, the other morning, Phillip had asked if I knew where he'd misplaced his blotter. Only someone with mental health issues would lose drugs in a house with children. I thought of the way spilled soup made him punch a hole in the closet door. And how only his battle with an inner demon could make him slap Jet for not posing for a photograph the way he planned.

"Yes. Yes, I'm sure he does," I answered.

"Can you get a note from your doctor?"

"He won't. I mean, he won't even go to couples counselling with me."

I'd asked him time and again. The last time he'd said no was also the last time I asked. I'd had the baby on my hip and Jet by the hand, decked out in a mermaid's tail I'd sewn from a shiny nylon housecoat and painted with blue scales to hide the flowers. The Mayne Island playgroup had spent weeks working on a Fall Fair float, gluing shells we'd gathered from the beach to pieces of driftwood so large we'd needed three men to lift them into the truck where all the kids would be sitting. Jet had practised waving and blowing kisses and expected us to be there, watching, waving, and blowing kisses back. Phillip cited a reason to do with the septic field for refusing to join us.

People on Mayne Island thought we were a happy couple because we drank at home together in front of the TV and didn't take turns at the bar like other couples, one drinking, the other staying home to watch the kids. Figuring his refusal had less to do with the septic field and more to do with a drinking buddy on his way over, I mentioned the idea of counselling once more. He glared at me, his silence following us out the door. Phillip didn't trust counsellors; he viewed them all as frauds.

When the baby was three months old, I began correspondence classes. Without the daycare subsidy I had to do my schoolwork from home, Maisie clinging to my breast like a leech while Jet pranced around in my old go-go boots and an Elvis cape decorated with gold glitter guitars, my university texts spread out on the bed—Spanish, French, English, philosophy, psychology—in a room that smelled of diapers.

The following year, in the fall of 2005, when Maisie was one and a half, I began making a weekly commute to the Victoria campus to study fiction. I was thirty-four years old, in a workshop with students young enough to be my children, being instructed by a poet, also younger than me, with tousled hair and a boyish grin.

Every Tuesday we'd leave Mayne Island on a morning ferry that sailed to Swartz Bay, a half-hour's drive from Victoria. I'd drive from the ferry terminal to my parents' house, hurriedly drop Maisie off with my mother, and then make it to the campus in time for class at one. As difficult as the commute was on my already strained relationship with Phillip, I never missed a class. And these weekly visits to Victoria helped me with my parents, although we never talked about my childhood.

Phillip thought my idea of moving to Victoria was preposterous. The townhouse for which I was wait-listed, right across the street from campus, had two bedrooms and a den. I planned to move the next year, with any luck before fall classes began in September of 2006. Phillip said he'd have nowhere to paint. Besides, "Don't you know what kind of weirdos there are on campus? You could be killed."

Weirdos on campus? How could Phillip really know me if he didn't know—didn't want to hear—about the years I'd spent dealing with "weirdos" every night?

Alone and lonely, waiting to begin my first full-time university term, I began to collect items from thrift stores and garage sales that I'd need in my new house. I acquired an armoire (from a Panamanian woman and her geologist husband), a metallic powder-blue 1960s sewing machine (free from the recycling depot), a Formica kitchen table and four grey chairs (I was *truly* leaving come next fall), bunk beds (mattresses included, from a friend who'd slept on them with his brothers and sisters since the eighties—do the multiplication: four kids over twenty years and no box springs—beggars couldn't be choosers), a heart-shaped wall lamp that glowed red, a wicker toy box that looked like an elephant, a small wooden shelf, a blue-painted sideboard for my clothes (its missing glass doors replaced with red and blue oilcloth), an almost complete set of yellow ceramic dishes (abandoned on the street), a half-dozen vintage coasters (free from the recycling depot), a cooking pot, a frying pan, a Dutch oven (that had once been used to do what, a craft? involving dyes? chemicals? The outside was splattered with irremovable paint and the inside smelled industrial when heated).

The futon with its frame was secondhand; it had sat in a little girl's basement playroom where she'd kept her toys. When the futon got too old, too covered with crayon marks, I bought it for fifty dollars. And that futon, more than any of the other pieces I collected, represented my newfound independence.

Since I'd brought it home it had acquired large stains of various shapes. That's because when I'd tried to manoeuvre it into our basement, along with the other things I'd collected there, it was too heavy for me and Phillip, in protest of my invading his studio space, wouldn't help. So I stored it on the front porch, where all summer our cat used it as a bed, leaving her fur and odour behind. A whole summer in which I knew the partnership was over. A whole summer in which Phillip did, too.

Then I ordered a cover for it from a designer factory in Toronto that specialized in retro designs—an indulgent, extravagant purchase that cost more than the futon itself. Pink barkcloth with green and white highlights and matching bolsters and cushions. A bold move in the direction of a better life.

The futon wasn't an expensive piece but it was a well-made one, its frame solid wood, not like the cheap tubular steel ones. That frame would survive an earthquake. And it was the one large piece of furniture that I'd be able to pass on to one of my children, that felt like it meant something, that would take up space in an empty room.

I may have planned the move but I was ad-libbing the lines, writing myself as I went along. After hearing former wards of the court might be eligible for funding, I began the process of accessing my court files. A few weeks later a brown manila envelope arrived in the mail. I read about myself in the third person—my arrests, my psychiatric evaluations, my social history; the multiple perspectives of police, psychiatrists, counsellors.

I read that my parents had put no effort into the reconciliation process. Their need to keep things private included a refusal to sign off on our family therapy records when a court-appointed psychologist asked for them. He wanted to speak to them; they refused to come in. Finally my father conceded to a phone call, in which he told the doctor that I'd been a difficult child who threw tantrums when she didn't get her way. He cited my jumping off monkey bars, the hard landings, as the reason for the bruises and scrapes on my body. He said that, jealous of my baby brother's arrival, I'd pinched him. Only the doctor saw the mysterious connection between these things.

My father wrote: "I, Paul Thanh, enter into an agreement for the care and custody of Yasuko Thanh, born June 30, 1971, for whom we have requested special care. Yasuko Thanh has the following disabilities/special needs: emotional instability requiring psychiatric treatment."

———

I thought about who I'd been.

I'd forgotten, or buried, much of my childhood and adolescence. When I thought of my parents I remembered the good times. The dried salted squid I savoured in Chinatown, a treat. Walking hand in hand with my father to the butcher who had Peking ducks hooked and hanging in his window. The scent of lavender on my pillow from a sachet my mother had made for me, shaped like a heart and stuffed with the bounty of her immaculate garden.

My own children were my life now.

I loved everything about them. The way Jet held an elastic in their mouth as they pulled up their hair into a ponytail. The way they asked "What's for dinner?" upon arriving home from school. How when the doctor entered Maisie's hospital room to withdraw a blood sample, Jet first tried to run away with her and then rocked her when it was over.

I loved the way Jet had retrieved everything Maisie pointed at until Maisie learned to walk. The way, when Maisie was a little older, she toddled after Jet, blessing the carpet with her sippy cup, sanctifying it with orange juice.

I loved their plays. Forty-five-minute extravaganzas. With costumes. Bunny ears drawn on white paper. Cut out and taped to Maisie's head. Whiskers drawn in washable felt tip. Jet as a witch with a long felt nose, fabric flowers pinned in their hair.

The lines Jet wrote on little pieces of paper:

"I am so sad since my wife died."

"He didn't see his daughter as much as he should because it painfulled him she was too much like her mother."

"She stole my beauty."

How, at the end of five acts—birth, death, jealousy, poisoning, coma—both children shredded the lines and threw the piles of paper up in the air.

Jet would write in my schoolbooks: "I love you. Even if I get taller than you."

They shared a room and sang "Gilligan's Island" to the tune of "Amazing Grace," sang, "One ton of metal" instead of "Guantanamera" at bedtime.

I even loved the way they fought.

"Give me a knife and I'll chop you into pieces of bacon," Maisie said.

Drumming their fingers, hands on their hips, in imitation of me, saying, "I'm down to my very last nerve with you. The very last."

But no one was ever banished for shouting in anger.

When Jet baked with me I'd bite down on my criticisms even when cookie dough was being flung across the room. I tried never to yell, even when I felt pulled in every direction like those sticky toys you threw at the wall shaped like an octopus, slithering down to end up behind the couch covered in dust or gerbil fur.

When they cried I sang to them. If I punished them at all, I used time-outs.

We discussed bad behaviour. Jet, wilful by nature, responded well to analogies.

"When a cop pulls you over, you want to kick him in the shins, right? But you don't. You'll go to jail. So you hand him your licence and smile and before you know it you're driving away. You don't have to feel respect," I said, "but you have to *show* it to your teachers, your counsellors. Heck, to me.

"Here's the thing: never forget to *be* a person you can respect."

The kids set their own bedtime. They ate potatoes one day, Duncan Hines icing the next, or left the table without finishing meals. My reactionary parenting was invisible to me.

One night we were talking about the Big Bopper Crash.

"You can hear the wind in the cornfield where the plane went down," Jet said.

"Does it sound like *labambalabambalabamba*?" Maisie said.

"No, it sounds like *whoosh*," I said.

"Well, maybe it does sound like La Bamba," Jet said. "If you listen very hard."

"And that's why we're SUPER GIRLS!" Maisie said.

"Goodnight monkey monsters. I love you."

"I love you. Banana pooh," they said together.

"I wonder what I'm going to be when I grow up," Jet said without warning.

"How about happy?"

Jet groaned. Maisie rolled her eyes.

"Be you."

I wanted my children to know—it was imperative they know—that they didn't have to *be* anything but themselves for me to love them.

Department of Heart Gouging

While at UVic, whenever I felt down I'd find a tattoo shop. I'd choose a large piece of work, giving myself a reason to return week after week. The prodding needles relaxed me. It wasn't that I was unhappy. Not exactly. Five courses, a new place I'd received word was mine and moved into days before the start of classes, two young children. Yet I found myself arriving at my fiction workshop without remembering how I got there. Or looking out the lecture-hall window at bare spots in the trees. Or, at home, down at the dining room table, dragging my fork through my mashed potatoes and making designs. After putting the kids to bed I'd spend time with my head in my hands, wondering what the hell was happening with my writing.

I'd gone from having a closed, private relationship with my work to setting it free among classmates who wielded Sharpies like swords. I told myself that courting the praise of others would only break my heart. That to become a better writer I needed to focus on my love affair with words. I feared others would look at me and say, "Who are you, anyway? What are you doing here? You don't belong."

By the following year, the autumn of 2007, the futon still smelled like a dirty cat, a woodsy musk tainted with a hint of death. The day's radiant sun giving way to a coastal evening chill heralded the beginning of my second year of full-time studies at UVic. By now I felt I'd developed a competent daily routine.

I was getting scholarships for my good grades, going to film festivals, writing, playing music. I was enjoying my children and the long last days of Indian summer at a lake before the clouds in all their West Coast glory consumed the rest of the blue sky. From our beach towels we threw seagulls potato chips and watched them pick at the sand by our feet.

So what the hell was I doing? Falling in love with an under-employed singer of country and western songs because he'd offered me his leather jacket as we'd smoked outside the pub after his show.

His name was Eddie. He was forty-one, in the middle of a divorce, working a call centre job he hated. Music was his love. I'd watched him perform that night, smiling stupidly in the audience, sure of my specialness and the world's abundance because of his baptizing gaze from the stage.

I told Eddie he should quit his job. The only thing keeping him from spending all his time making music was his rent—and if he moved in with me he could work on his recordings as much as he wanted. He hesitated. To be working defined him. I needed to change his outlook. Let him know that there were many ways to contribute, not only financially. I set out to convince him with the same intensity with which I approached my university assignments.

I argued that he was already spending every night with me. He'd arrive back at my place after his shift at the call centre where he fielded complaints for a cellular phone company, have dinner with me and the children at the kitchen table. Typically, the children and I sat watching cartoons on the computer while we ate. Now the computer was turned off and we faced each other over our food.

Mornings, he'd borrow my car to drive himself back out to work, a thirty-minute commute.

I considered this a victory. If he had my car, he'd have to return. I could do without it. Especially if it meant that our relationship was growing stronger, more solid.

"You make me feel peaceful," I said. "I sleep better when you're here."

I viewed the time he spent apart from me as a minor infidelity. He lived in a bachelor suite on the Gorge, a few blocks from where I'd once lived with the trio of bikers in a building from the fifties with a view of the water, the lingering odour of tobacco smoke in the air. He'd decorated his walls with photographs of famous people he'd met, rockabilly Hall of Famers, movie stars from the forties, pin-ups who were now in their seventies and still toured the circuit. They'd ended up in many of the places he played, like Viva Las Vegas, the largest rockabilly music festival in the world and a pilgrimage site for those like Eddie who lived as though it was still the fifties. Women and men who never listened to music more recent than Elvis. Who wore vintage clothing. Who cooked recipes from old magazines, things like aspic, as their grand-mothers had.

I identified with the subculture in idealizing this "simpler time," imagining rows of houses with tidy picket fences where nothing bad ever happened.

The dream could be mine.

If he moved in.

My need spurred a methodology that involved reminding him of how much he hated his job, of his wish to spend all his time making music. Then underlining it with our mortality, the limited time on earth we had to achieve anything. The goal was less to help him fulfill his ambitions than to make him mine.

Impelling my project were notions like these: We aren't "seri-ous" if we don't live together. If he loved me, he'd spend every spare second with me. His things at my place signify that he can no longer walk out of our relationship without warning.

My life was the upward climb, the frantic grasp at anything I could hold, a rock, a branch, that would save my life.

I was desperate without knowing it.

I chose not to focus on the things about him that irritated me: a penchant for seeing the glass half full, a sense of entitlement that translated into a view of the world as unfair. I dwelled instead on my age, my fading beauty. I told myself, This is your last chance to snag a good man.

I concentrated on the smallest things he did with the children as evidence that he'd make a perfect stepfather.

I dismissed the fact that we had no intellectual connection—university filled that need. That our emotional bond ran shallow was written off by correlating "depth" with pretension. Who wanted to mine their psyche when they could dance on its glistening surface?

I was, once again, subsuming important aspects of my character to build a connection with a man. I called it love. It was fear.

On the day he moved his furniture and boxes in, I finally had proof. That we were really a couple, meant to be together.

The stacks of boxes reached the ceiling and were five feet deep in places.

He looked helplessly at the mess. "Don't worry," I said, "by the time you get home from work these piles won't be here."

I rearranged everything in my tiny storage locker. Moved my things from the living room into other rooms, recreated my space to absorb and accommodate his.

I didn't think of my children.

I ignored the detail that a couch in the kitchen—his vintage seven-foot-long couch—made half the room unreachable. That the area where my children watched movies and played with their toys would become a chamber for his guitars.

How the hell was it that I'd gotten out of one relationship and, within months of meeting another man—in a bar at that—I was living with him?

When he strummed his vintage Gretsch on stage women flocked to him, were transformed. Suddenly you could be a jazzy type walking some slick city sidewalk in New York with a little dog on a red leash. You could be someone crazy riding a zip line. His music made that possible. Bombshell beauties with hourglass figures pseudo-stripteased on the dance floor as they tried to catch his eye. In my mind, every woman in every club he played in was conniving to steal him from me. I'd pinch myself, scratch myself under the table, under my skirt, until I bled—to punish myself for the attention he gave them.

My mind spun justifications for my behaviour from any shred of evidence I could find that he must be cheating—a smile, a handshake, a hug. My heart racing, my breath jagged, I'd look to see if he had an erection hidden beneath his suit.

Insecurity consumed me. I dyed my hair black to hide the grey at my roots, bought new dresses from the thrift store, made up my face with the concentration of an artist before I'd even leave the house with him.

My biggest fear was that he'd tire of me. Cheat on me with a groupie. Every woman became the prostitute I'd been, who'd use any tactic to seduce a man.

My true heart was telling me to get out. Learn to make my own way. Forge a future for myself by myself.

My heart was telling me that my low self-esteem was a curse. A literal spell cast by an enemy who wanted me out of the picture.

After Eddie moved in our tiny townhouse no longer felt like home, crammed with too much stuff, my computer desk against the kitchen wall blocked by that seven-foot couch.

Forget the table where the four of us, to my delight, had eaten our meals when he still had his apartment. These days it was simpler to eat dinner cross-legged with a plate on your lap on the carpet, anywhere with a square inch of room. Rows of records snaked down the hallway; books lined the walls like balustrades. Every closet was stacked to the ceiling so that coats and shoes and boots found themselves pushed out of their home, cluttering the floor from the front door to the back. The futon still anchored the living room but was difficult to find behind the bass and guitar amps, mic stands, patch cords, stage lights.

In the winter of 2008, we moved to a bungalow twice the size down the street. The yard stretched around the house in a half-acre rectangle, which at its centre, according to the gardener, the biggest sumac tree on Vancouver Island. I had a view of the ocean, and double the expenses

"I promise, I'll get another job," Eddie said. Instead he was let go from the one he had.

I got two flaming anchors tattooed on my chest above the names of my children. I wanted to be anchored. By my children, by love. I successfully applied for a research grant to write a book of short stories with a historical component. *Historiography*, I'd written in my application.

At UVic, I had an instructor who was brilliant at creating individual exercises to break the idiosyncratic habits each student's writing tended toward. A student who wrote only third-person, past-tense stories was asked to write a piece in the present tense from the first-person point of view. Another, who relied too heavily on exposition, was asked not to use any at all. Since my writing tended toward the cryptic, the axiomatic, the structurally experimental, i.e., confusing without purpose, he asked me to write a story with a linear structure and scenes of no less than three pages each, in chronological order.

As I wrote, I felt as though I were simply recording. As though I'd gone from being a "writer" to a "reporter." Feeling pedantic, I finished the short story I called "Floating Like the Dead." The premise was based on true events, the quarantining of Chinese lepers on an island visible from Cordova Bay, a short drive up the street from my house.

I sent the story off and had it rejected, more than once, before it found a home in a now-defunct magazine, *The Vancouver Review*, during the spring of 2009.

To my surprise, the editor told me she'd like to submit my story to the Journey Prize contest—the yearly anthology of shortlisted stories on the cutting edge of Canadian literature. How absurd— yet sweet—that they should think of submitting my piece.

In comparison to other stories I'd written, I didn't think this one shone.

To my further surprise, the story made the top three. Then it ended up winning the prize for "the best short story published in Canada" in 2009.

Was everyone nuts? I couldn't believe the win had anything to do with the strength of my writing. The characters were Chinese, and I had an Asian name. I was a member of a visible minority, and a woman, and had pointed out the historical racism of my region and its apathy. I concluded that the story had won only because it was politically correct.

Swept up in a maelstrom of readings, I couldn't breathe. My lack of confidence made me undeserving of everything that was happening to me. At any moment I'd stumble. At any moment the dream would be yanked away. Forced into the public eye, I verged on vomiting and shook from the podium. I craved the safe anonymity of my living room, the boundaries of whatever story I was writing and hiding in, at a table in sunlight. I no longer belonged to the streets. I didn't belong in this artistic, intellectual milieu either.

I came home from Toronto, where the prize ceremony had been held, to find a message on my machine from one of Canada's best agents. Denise Bukowski was a rock star of the literary world. For years, reading authors' acknowledgments, I'd been seeing her name.

Professionally, things were looking up: after the Journey Prize, a contract with McClelland & Stewart, a book deal, a short story collection that would be published in 2012. Personally, they were worsening.

I told Eddie about my pain, my past. It hurt to have him respond that everyone's pain was the same.

"No one pushed me through high school," he said in a misguided attempt at understanding. "So I didn't get the last credit I needed."

How is your not finishing high school like feeling the world would be better off without me? I thought. What I said was "Lots of people never finished high school. Including the producer of *60 Minutes*," hoping Eddie would stop dwelling on what he didn't have, exaggerating his lack of education as a fatal flaw that excused him from not going after what he claimed to want: better paying, more rewarding work.

And yet. In the summer of 2010, we married. The date was June 27, three days before my thirty-ninth birthday. He landed a job that allowed him to contribute half the rent and bills. But he kept using my student-loan money to cut albums and print up gig posters.

From the fall of 2011 to the spring of 2012, I tutored, worked as a teaching assistant, marked papers, trying to paddle my way out of the vortex. Eddie lost his job, and the months when I failed to make ends meet, I'd vow that Maisie would keep up her gymnastics lessons no matter what, even if I had to return to the sex trade to pay for them. I'd sit through her two-hour class simply because my parents never had, as if they were at fault for my financial situation, as if my presence in the viewing box could set things right. I'd watch Maisie through the glass, clapping at her cartwheels, cheering—I'd be the kind of parent that nurtured, that paid for the cello, the saxophone, the flute lessons, the private music teacher, the band trip. No matter what, I'd do the opposite of what my parents had done. Then a writing gig would come along and save me from the brink of disaster.

When I began slipping from my own expectations as a mother, I turned a dark corner. Believing I'd failed, I became convinced that my presence on earth was harming my children. I was a murderer. Nothing anyone said could persuade me I wasn't killing them slowly. A harmless comment made about Maisie forgetting to say please drove me to my basement office, where I shut the door to burn my arms with a lighter until they blistered. I'd julienne the blister open with a paper clip. Rub cinders from my overflowing ashtray into the wound as if seasoning ground beef, then pour whisky onto it in preparation for another flambé.

I heard voices in my head. Music, Christmas songs of all things, that kept me up and whose volume I tried to lower by picturing a stereo and turning down the knob. It didn't work, despite the sedatives I'd take like candy. Once asleep, I couldn't stay asleep for long. Food tasted wrong; I couldn't swallow it. And I gradually came to feel that my parents, who to keep us from starving had begun dropping off groceries every Tuesday—loonie-store chili, discount bread—were trying to poison me.

——

Here a psychiatrist could step in and point to how the symptoms of borderline personality disorder may include paranoid delusions under stress. These grafted themselves to the Asian half of me—the half that believed in curses, demons, bad spirits, hungry ghosts, shape-shifting devils who took on human form and acted as conduits for bad luck and diseases, like Typhoid Mary. Comorbidities like psychotic depression leapt on board the bandwagon like circus monkeys.

I was working too hard, eating and sleeping too little, and stressed about money. My simmering resentment of Eddie, who'd left me holding the bag, went unexpressed, my desperate need for him preventing my voicing any objections. Then everything grew worse when Donna, Eddie's adult stepdaughter with his ex-wife, moved to town. She'd been living in Washington State but had lost the green card lottery.

My first book, which also formed my master's thesis, had come out in April, 2012, and by June of that same year, I'd started work on my next book, a novel.

"Why is she coming?" I asked.

Her Canadian driver's licence needed to be renewed.

He'd told her he'd get her a job. Help her get settled. Do anything she needed until she found a place of her own. Amid my turmoil I couldn't understand what moving to Victoria had to do with renewing her licence.

"What's Donna's relationship like with her mom?" I asked Eddie. "Did she leave on her own or was she asked to leave? I'm just trying to wrap my mind around it because—and I don't mean to sound cold—but I can tell you that never, never in a million years would

I let Maisie or Jet move to some town you and your new woman were living in."

"I don't think I'm insignificant to the kids."

I knew he was. Relatively. I thought back to all the times I'd encouraged Maisie to respond to his jokes. Asked Jet to do me the favour of saying good morning or goodnight to him. Bought Eddie a birthday card for the children to sign. Asked them, for my sake, to repeat a story they'd heard in school or to recount what had happened on the playground. The way they'd grudgingly comply, the way they avoided eye contact at the dinner table, broke my heart.

As did the way I tried to elicit praise from him on the children's behalf. "Look, honey, isn't that a great cartwheel Maisie just did?" "Jet got an A on the science quiz. Isn't that wonderful?" "Hon, have you noticed Maisie's hair?" "Doesn't Jet look cool today?"

I was convinced that, if not for my efforts, days would go by without their interacting at all. That was the true curse: there was no practical reason why they should. It was Mom who got breakfast ready. Mom who got Maisie dressed for school, who got her there and back, helped with homework, gave her a bath, read the stories, put her to bed.

Donna wanted to be picked up at the airport, saying she didn't think she could manage all her bags. Practical women carried backpacks. How else could they negotiate the jungles of Borneo, the hills of Cambodia?

Besides, it was my birthday. I was turning forty-one. My father had made dinner reservations weeks before.

"Go without me," Eddie said.

I sat with Jet and Maisie and my parents in the sushi restaurant, trying to celebrate. My heart wasn't in it, especially when my father asked "Where's Eddie?" with an admixture of judgment and concern.

When we got home Maisie was still awake. I'd hoped the car ride would put her to sleep, relieving me for once from her nightly bedtime rituals. Even as a baby she'd disliked change, but lately her need of routine had morphed into a strict adherence to compulsions that had to be performed. Ten bathroom trips. Touch the stickers she'd put on her headboard, "One, two, three . . ." Like a pony on a merry-go-round she'd circle the room to open and close the blinds, the closet door, the cupboards of her craft shelf, riveted to a track from which she couldn't escape. Measuring her mattress, making and remaking the bed, five storybooks read in a certain order. Her stuffies lined up according to a design only she and the workers who lived in her ceiling knew or understood. If any step was omitted, any one done wrong, the ride would start again from the very beginning.

Eddie had noticed that Maisie's OCD got worse when I was around. Either I was the cause or I enabled her rituals. The conclusion in either case: I was a shitty mom.

I remembered my own childhood compulsions to count or touch things, yet I never made the conscious link between my history and Maisie's symptoms. Each night she and I would be up till two a.m.—appeasing the workers who had cameras, who recorded everything, who checked their video surveillance for mistakes. Seven or eight hours of "getting things right."

Maisie's bedroom window looked over our front yard with its ornamental cherry tree that blossomed so profusely people would stop to take a photograph. Snow globes were arrayed on her orange-painted dresser that my mother had stencilled with green gecko designs. From her ceiling hung a turquoise mesh organizer holding silver dress-up shoes the length of my palm, feather boas, tutus, my old gymnastics bodysuits. Her life was beautiful. What was driving her behaviour?

I scoured the internet for information. Bought two books online, *Talking Back to OCD* and *What to Do When Your Brain Gets Stuck*. I tried practising cognitive behavioural therapy with her. *If you're afraid of spiders, sit with one in your lap.*

As art and life fed off each other, the protagonist of the novel I was working on—tentatively titled *Mysterious Fragrance of the Yellow Mountains*—began seeing and hearing things, began believing the world was poisoning her. Salvation came in the form of her baby, born golden and glowing with magical protective powers. Scenes that I later cut from the book.

That birthday night, I experienced such violent anger about Donna's arrival that I wanted to kill everyone around me. And now Maisie stood in her room, still naked from her shower, terrified of going to bed: her sheets were crooked. I tried to straighten them, but when I didn't succeed she screamed "I have nails in my head!" Then she ran outside with no clothes on and hid behind a bush, in the dark, in the cold. That settled it.

I made an appointment with our family doctor, who referred us to Saanich Child and Youth Mental Health. We were added to the waiting list while I fought a worsening battle with the bars holding Maisie prisoner, and my own despair when all I could do was share her cell. I'd struggle to grasp her fists so that she wouldn't punch herself, to pin her arms to her sides while I'd yell "Leave her alone!" at the ceiling. SCYMH couldn't tell me the cavalry's ETA, when a psychiatrist would be available.

Three weeks later, they called to say we'd been fast-tracked through the system. We had an appointment.

Maisie and I sat down with Dr. Nixon, a pediatric psychiatrist, who pried apart the two sides of a plastic toy brain to show Maisie where hers was broken. She explained the function of her hippocampus, her thalamus, her orbital frontal cortex. She took Maisie's finger and had her point at the centre, where her striatum lay.

"This is your caudate nucleus. Right now it's like a malfunctioning stoplight. But the exciting part is—we can fix it."

Maisie was diagnosed with pediatric obsessive-compulsive disorder and put on a course of psychotropic treatment: Prozac medication titrated to a dose large enough to put a horse to sleep.

I had faith in her psychiatrist. But my own obsession, centred on the originating thought that I'd been cursed—by who? a fan of Eddie's?—only grew stronger, like a river that rises with the melting snow to quit her banks. Impossible to fight with sandbags of rationality.

Before Eddie had moved in with all his stuff, before Maisie became sick, she and Jet had happily played on the futon, lying on its pink barkcloth cover, floating on its pale green and yellow polka dots. With Maisie's head in the crook of Jet's arm, Jet would read to her from picture books; or, head to foot, they'd watch cartoons on the tiny pink TV I'd bought to match.

Eddie hadn't asked whether it was okay for him to lend the futon to Donna.

I was not insane. Unlike Picasso—who refused to donate used clothing to strangers and once beat his wife for giving away an old sweater instead of burning it—I'd contributed children's clothing to the Salvation Army, toys to the church-run thrift store. And I preferred buying my own clothes secondhand.

But Eddie's lending out my futon shook my tenuous hold on reality. Maisie's OCD became part of what I now saw as a broad-spectrum evil eye that had hexed me as well as my children.

"It has to be your ex-wife," I said to Eddie one night in bed.

"What the what-what?" He didn't look up from his book, a paperback copy of a Tom Petty biography he'd picked up from a garage sale.

"The futon. Because you lent it to Donna. And your ex-wife. She's trying to break us up from afar."

In my head, the connection between my depression, Maisie's OCD, his ex-wife, his stepdaughter, and the futon was crystal clear.

Frustrated, Eddie wondered what was wrong with me and what I wanted him to do about it.

Find me a counter-curse, I wanted to say.

I knew that no generic version would work. Apart from those hokey websites that sold crystals and essential oils and bats' feet, there were no guidebooks for what I wanted, no lists of instructions.

I purified the house with incense. I burned candles, opened windows to let the demons out. I swept breadcrumbs and hair-balls and rogue cherry blossoms as though evil could be cleansed with a dustpan and elbow grease.

I asked Eddie, "If a zombie bit me would you shoot me or tie me to a post in the backyard?"

"If I were a quadriplegic would you stay with me?"

"If I'd been on the *Titanic* would you have risked your life to save mine?"

I tried the impossible: to measure degrees of love.

I needed him to be the kind of man who'd throw himself on top of me when the shooting began.

I filled my day with tasks: to keep my mind from stumbling, I scrubbed the kitchen until the house smelled of bleach, yanked dandelions, stopped Maisie from bashing out her brains on her headboard and screaming at two a.m., knowing that Jet had to get up at five for a paper route. Still, my already shaky grasp of reality began slipping like fried eggs from a greasy plate.

Meanwhile we celebrated Jet's birthday, Maisie, Jet, and I, by going to the lake and having corn dogs for dinner. I hid my delusions from my classmates, my children, their friends, their parents. I was known as the mom who'd host a party for twenty, parents dropping their kids off at my door with looks of astonishment overwritten by doubt. "Are you sure you know what you're doing?"

"Oh, yeah," I'd say, winking, "we got this."

Jet's friends called me the "cool" mom because I'd rent them movies and then drift around, offering bowls of chips and slices of pizza.

"And then he was like, We only made out for like three seconds and—"

"Don't you like how like every time you hear something that's bad about a guy that you like—"

"And, like, that time I was with Brian on the phone?"

"Oh, my god."

"Do you know what my favourite thing is, when we're in the Pharmasave and he starts singing? Have you actually heard him sing? Yeah, he's such a great stylist."

I let them eat chocolate brownies for dinner. Hot Wings and Dill Pickle chips for dessert.

———

I burst into tears at my doctor's office when she asked me whether stepping in front of a bus seemed like an appropriate solution.

I wept in relief. Oh, yes. Yes. And if a zombie tried to eat me, I'd turn the other cheek. And if I was on the *Titanic* with my children, I'd hold them tight and welcome the water as it covered us.

As she returned from the photocopier with my prescription I mentioned how I'd always thought I was stronger than people who needed meds to survive.

I was working on revisions to my latest draft of *Mysterious Fragrance of the Yellow Mountains.*

My validation and success as a writer were enabling me to provide for my children, giving me the opportunity to meet my literary heroes at readings and festivals. The self-harm and the psychotic breaks battled my new image of myself.

I couldn't reconcile honouring my past with overcoming it.

Sleepless, I argued with my delusions of persecution.

Screaming Torture and Administrative Errors

A few months later my doctor added Topiramate to my Escital-opram prescription, but the stereo in my head remained, just tuned to a different channel.

The doctor switched my Escitalopram for Citalopram, another antidepressant, then raised my dosage.

But the pitch at which I was falling had grown too steep. I flapped my arms with the wings she'd given me, continuing to fall like a broken bird getting nowhere.

We were kicked out of our house when the owners sold it the same month my agent placed my novel with Penguin Random House during the spring of 2014. I got drunk as often as I could to numb a new delusion: that Eddie was in on a plot to kill me along with my parents.

I had nowhere to go, no one to turn to, I took cover in a corner of the basement. Out of sight, protected by the boxes Eddie had stored there, behind hangers full of winter coats and balls of tangled Christmas lights.

Like Dorothy clicking the heels of her sparkly red shoes, I begged to go home. I opened my eyes; I was still in the basement. I wept bitterly. I drew my knees to my chest and rocked.

By that October, I'd received revision notes from my publisher, and was working on incorporating them, and I'd begun to think, As soon as the book comes out. As soon as it wins a prize. As soon as my agent sells U.S. rights. Exactly what would happen then I wasn't sure, but I kept my handle on these feelings as though clutching the hilt of a sword.

Then my body got sick. It hurt too much to eat and I lost weight, dropping to eighty-six pounds. Pain curled me into a ball. Ulcers, my doctor said. Kidney infection.

I'd been on strong antibiotics for a few days when, in the middle of a tutoring session, I collapsed.

The hospital ran tests, ultrasounds. My gall bladder had swelled to the size of a banana and verged on bursting. I would have to wait three days in hospital for my surgery. On my first night, yet to be placed in a room on a ward, on a gurney in a hospital hallway, high on morphine, I recalled through a drug-induced fog what would happen—something good—as soon as the book came out. I moved my IV cord out of the way, struggled to prop myself up, then scribbled editing notes onto a hard copy of the manuscript.

I wrote because Eddie couldn't pay the bills.

I wrote because I selfishly expected him to.

I wrote because I loved my children.

I wrote because when I finished the book nothing bad would ever happen to me again.

On my return from the hospital, I slept with a kitchen knife. Unable to protect myself or my children, arming myself gave me peace of mind.

Mysterious Fragrance of the Yellow Mountains explored themes of resilience, transcendence: not what I had, but what I needed. Complications following surgery on my liver and pancreas resulted in more tests that finally explained what had happened to my body in the first place: eosinophilia. The blood cells tasked with killing parasites, or cancer, had in confusion attacked my organs. Thankfully, the part of my body at war with the rest had launched its assault against my digestive organs and not my heart. The irony of my own body trying to put me out of my misery did not escape me.

I needed strength. I needed an antidepressant and a mood stabilizer to get through the day. I needed to read my novel and love it. I needed to stay in bed but I didn't have the freedom to be sick, the luxury of having another pull the rope for a while.

As a mother, I felt myself succumbing to my body's weakness, dizziness, nausea, as if to an undertow when you've grown too tired to swim. In the glass viewing booth at Maisie's gym I'd daydream about how my children would be much happier after I was gone. I was dying anyway. In between the chapters I was revising I researched shooting, hanging, jumping, overdosing.

All I had to do was finish the book, then I could let go.

After the book was published, I left Jet, who was by now seventeen, in charge of Maisie and the house, and went to Vancouver, locking myself into a Downtown Eastside hotel room. Smoked cigarettes out of my fourth-floor window, too exhausted, borderline contemptuous, to write. Then I walked down an alley to buy drugs. I lost my room key and asked the desk clerk for another.

The squalor outside the hotel was matched by the dingy lobby. One door led to a bar with sticky floors opposite dirty picture windows and a ridiculous seating arrangement consisting of threadbare couches no one in their right mind would want to sit on. Not to mention the view: people camped on the sidewalk in front of tarps that cradled their useless wares—single shoes, clasp-less necklaces, bruised fruit, things fished out of dumpsters and bartered for drugs.

The clerk stood behind the counter in a suit jacket, subverting its propriety with his choker necklace of prison tattoos.

He said, "How will you get to your room now? Fly?" He had a heavy European accent. He had silver teeth.

I told him he was cheeky.

He yanked my arm over the counter so hard my eyes watered. "Cheeky? What means cheeky?"

His name was Vlady. He was flirting with me. I knew he was flirting in the language we spoke—that all of us spoke, the broken who'd had to fight for every single thing they owned, who'd gone hungry, who knew how to get a thing done, who punished themselves harder than anyone else, who'd shaken off the dust of the past, who'd moved through valleys of death without expecting God to step in, who'd toyed with pain. He clutched my wrist, understanding that I needed to be touched.

Then he laughed.

He let go of my wrist and handed me a new key. For a moment, I'd felt safe.

I went up to my room. 408. Flopped down on the bed. The dresser was littered with sesame balls I hadn't eaten; they sat on brown butcher paper slick with grease, the room stank of them, and of whisky, empty bottles overflowing the trash can. On the windowsill were half-empty Styrofoam cups of coffee from the lobby swimming with cigarette butts, one knocked over, a fetid brown lake dotted by tobacco-filter islands. Not even a fly would live in such filth. I lay there staring at the cracks on the ceiling, yellow with nicotine and age, thinking about all the things I'd wanted from Eddie, for my children.

I took a shower and my hands, soaping my flesh, were meat, my body, irrelevant. I had no affection for my breasts, my thighs. Even my memories—the children's birth, their parties, their laughter— I viewed with detachment.

I got out of the shower and lay back down on the bed soaking wet. The *tap-tap-tap* of the old-fashioned radiator made me think of wrestlers, tapping and tapping and tapping each other out on the mat. Hulk Hogan switching places with Jake the Snake when he was too tired to go on.

I'd severed the cord connecting my spirit to my body, the mechanical tapping of my heart, the numb rattle of my breath, the echo of a migraine. *Tap. Tap. Tap.* I had one thing left to do.

In 1941 Virginia Woolf wrote a note to her husband, weighed her pockets with stones, then drowned herself in the River Ouse. I needed to head to the Ivanhoe, fill my pockets with scrap metal, and walk into the Fraser along whose banks I'd once written poetry. Terrible poems.

Thomas Mann believed that one might remain as sick as possible without actually dying.

I had a choice. Or did I? Light cycled into darkness. Everything became its opposite in time.

———

The doctors at the Urgent Short Term Assessment and Treatment service sent a team to take me to the psyche ward. I was admitted to the Archie Courtnall Centre, home of the insane, the loony bin. A nurse took my clothes, wallet, shoelaces, cigarettes. The bathrooms had no shower curtains and I wasn't allowed a toothbrush. They gave me two new medications, including an antipsychotic, meant to help me tell the difference between fantasy and reality. *Meds.*

People who needed them used that word.

"What kind of meds are you on?"

Or, "I heard they had to switch her meds—the last ones didn't work."

Or, the worst one of all, "He did it because he was *off his meds.*"

For hours I stared at a leaf and, the next day, a wall. It was peaceful here. People played their demons close to the hip. Even when being strapped down to a gurney. This building was so old that everyone slept with ghosts. The memories our bodies held flowed around and through us, nothing sturdy underfoot.

By the time I was released a few days later, Eddie had moved his furniture out of the house. I stood quietly in the middle of the empty living room, looking at my children—who sat in the mess left behind, cross-legged on the hardwood floor, encircled by scattered books and the dishes he'd removed from the sideboard—and felt furious. Furious enough to fake a smile and say "Hey. Let's go for ice cream."

As we headed out I spotted a spider on the door frame. Spiders meant luck. A spider in the house meant money was on the way. She was spinning her sack; she was building up venom. I watched in horror as my own hand smacked her with my purse, the squashed remains of her body clinging to the wood. The precision and speed with which injury could be inflicted by the powerful.

As soon as they knew, friends took charge. A couple I knew brought boxes of their grandmother's dishes, pint mugs and wine-glasses, coffee and end tables they'd been meaning to sell but "Now you can have them. No, don't worry. Don't pay us. They weren't doing us any good anyway." A friend helped me make lists of what I still needed, drove me to pawnshops and thrift stores, helped me track down the best sideboard, arranging for its delivery when I stood at the cash register, too stunned to make sense of the paperwork.

During our final days together Eddie had returned my futon, the wooden frame I'd thought would withstand an earthquake broken, the cover with its happy polka dots stained. No longer sharing the bedroom, I'd tossed and turned on its narrow width, my office too small to unfold it. Now friends heaved the unwieldy frame through the garage door, wrestled it up the staircase outside and then down the hall into the living room to fill the emptiness Eddie left behind. I'd been right about one thing: it did take up space in a room.

The therapist wanted me to say "I deserve love," but I began to weep instead. I'd long ago decided that to make it in this life you had to be tough.

That discipline, tenacity, ambition, talent, resourcefulness, and hard work were no guarantee of success.

That no one *deserved* anything, not a shot, not a fair shake.

Not for being born.

Not gymnastics lessons.

Not their parents' attention.

Not even love.

She questioned me. Why had I ended up where I did? What made me crazy, what made me self-punish when I failed at a task? I wrote in the hope of finding answers, but what I couldn't let go of, and what couldn't let go of me, continued to haunt.

PART III

CIRCLE OF RETURN

TORONTO, 2016. I'm in a theatre downtown, sitting on a not-uncomfortable chair in a row close to the stage.

My editor tucked a strand of glossy brown hair behind her ear. I'd heard she was the youngest woman to have been the president of a major publishing company in Canada. I'd also heard she missed important business meetings to bake chocolate chip cookies with her sons. She impressed me.

Penguin sold bestsellers, but she spoke as if money were the least of her concerns. Like anyone, I'm sure she hoped for good profits, which could then go toward the advances paid to unknown authors like me. Books—the art of them—excited her, and with her voice racing, with hand gestures that would impress any Italian, she championed her favourites.

A cheongsam collar decorated the front of my dress, jazzing up what would otherwise have been a plain cotton number. I could still taste the wine I'd finished in the lobby before ushers herded us in here, the theatre, for the beginning of the award ceremony. I flipped through the Writers' Trust Prize program, scanning the shortlist, the bios of nominees, including my own.

The week before, the partnered TV studio had clipped mics to the collars of each fiction writer and filmed them as they read their books' opening lines; computer magic had added their covers floating in virtual space to the left of our heads. I stuttered in answer to the questions producers had prepared to preface my book. Watching it now on a twenty-foot screen, it was impossible for me not to criticize my appearance: frown lines, crow's feet, the bun in my hair. All eyes were turned to the emcee, who was introducing the plot.

"Here we go," my editor said. Sitting next to her, my publicist gave me an encouraging nod.

I'd already received a large advance in three instalments. I'd put the money into my credit union account, where, thanks to online banking, I could visit my balance from the comfort of my bedroom.

My agent had worked tirelessly to secure me a living wage. Only now, in my forties, did pride sneak into my view of my work. I'd closed the file months back and celebrated with a bologna sandwich and whisky. The bliss spread like a taproot in my backyard, ideas multiplying like irises I'd planted under the cherry tree; I smiled at those expert gardeners, my agent, my publicist, my editor, sitting nearly close enough to me for comfort. I was a survivor. I held my breath without meaning to as the emcee in his suit and tie read out the list of books against which I was competing for the $25,000 Rogers Writers' Trust Prize. This was part of the job, hoping without dwelling, however good or bad the outcome.

In less than six months I'd gone from a bed in a psyche ward to a luxury hotel with a TV in the bathroom mirror.

One month from now I'd begin work on another book, a memoir.

Now, unable to sit still in my little black dress, I had the strange sense that my life had prepared me for this moment.

I thought of all I'd been through to get here. The beatings, the rapes. The serial affairs falling one after another like dominoes. Maisie's OCD, her journey with meds. My journey with meds. My attempt to mediate with parents who'd given me everything they had yet still failed to provide what I'd needed. I saw them as they were then, young, hopeful, eyes glinting with mischief, hands held in love, and I saw them as they were today, a world of two, wrinkled warriors, living in the cloistered shelter of the rooms in which I'd grown up.

As the emcee opened the white envelope containing the winner's name, I remember thinking that I was lucky. I remember thinking that, win or lose, I'd written a book. That nothing could hurt me now.

ACKNOWLEDGMENTS

THIS BOOK IS FOR THOSE WHO WERE THERE, and for those who are no longer with us. I'd like to thank 12 Midnite for his courage, loyalty, and enduring compassion, Fiona Lam, Jane Silcott, Zoey Leigh Peterson, Anakana Schofield for teaching me what it means to bear witness, Caroline Adderson, Suzie Spitfyre, Stéphane Gagnon, and Anastasia Andrews. I thank my agent, Denise Bukowski, for her steadfast faith in me, and my editor and publisher, Nicole Winstanley, for reading me like a soul sister. Thank you Shaun Oakey and Karen Alliston for line edits. For always being there, I'd like to thank Yvette Guigueno, Terry Glavin, and Andrew Struthers. Thank you to my children Jet and Maisie, and a special thank-you to Mick Garris.

In remembrance of Lucky, Lebanese Sam, Barrington (Buzz) Beswick, Royce, Kimi, Brandy, Sarah, and Toby.

Portions of this book have appeared in the following publications: *Prairie Fire*, *Vancouver Noir* (anthology), *Love Me Do* (anthology), *Taddle Creek*, *SUBterrain*, *Speak: Journalists for Human Rights*, and *Walk Me Home* (anthology).

The author wishes to acknowledge the support of the B.C. Arts Council, the Canada Arts Council, and The Writers' Trust.

A NOTE ABOUT THE TYPE

Mistakes to Run With is set in Monotype Van Dijck, a face originally designed by Christoffel van Dijck, a Dutch typefounder (and sometime goldsmith) of the seventeenth century. While the roman font may not have been cut by van Dijck himself; the italic, for which original punches survive, is almost certainly his work. The face first made its appearance circa 1606. It was re-cut for modern use in 1937.